That's the Way I Think

That's the Way I Think

Dyslexia and dyspraxia explained

David Grant

With illustrations by
Hannah Evelyn French

 David Fulton Publishers

David Fulton Publishers Ltd
The Chiswick Centre, 414 Chiswick High Road,
London W4 5TF

First published in Great Britain in 2005 by David Fulton
Publishers

10 9 8 7 6 5 4 3 2 1

www.fultonpublishers.co.uk

David Fulton Publishers is a division of Granada
Learning Limited, part of ITV plc.

British Library Cataloguing in Publication Data
A Catalogue record for this book is available from the
British Library.

ISBN 1 84312 375 4

Typeset by RefineCatch Limited, Bungay, Suffolk
Printed and bound in Great Britain

Contents

Foreword

For many years, the academic and motor movement aspects of dyslexia and dyspraxia were the main focuses of interest and hence of reading material produced for educators, parents and learners themselves. Much has been published on these features, and particularly on accepted, current teaching methodologies. In more recent years, information has been disseminated that has linked the frustration of those living and studying with these conditions to stress and anxiety.

In this book, David Grant has taken the understanding of dyslexia and dyspraxia in young people that one stage further – by linking it to lifestyle. He explains what it feels like to live with dyslexia and/or dyspraxia and how these conditions impact on thinking, feeling and functioning in situations beyond the classroom.

Once young people have been identified as having one or both of these conditions, they often feel relieved, as they know that there is a legitimate reason for any difficulties experienced in the learning process. The fear of being labelled 'lazy' or 'intellectually incapable' dissipates with understanding. There are many other aspects of life, however, that also need to be understood. This book will hopefully begin to lift the clouds of confusion on some of those facets, as individuals learn more about themselves. It will be heartening for people to realise that so many of the situations that cause them anxiety are quite common and that they are not the only ones experiencing often quite significant challenges! The case-studies cited are a useful tool in this process.

Further, the clarity with which David Grant writes will hopefully enable some young people to begin to describe their own circumstances and confidently advocate for themselves within the education system, at home and ultimately in the workplace.

I am sure that this book will be read by many and that it will bring understanding and hope where currently there is confusion and fear. David Grant has set out to engender a deeper personal understanding about dyslexia and dyspraxia – he has succeeded.

Dr Lindsay Peer CBE
Chartered Psychologist and
International Dyslexia Consultant
Former Education Director and
Deputy CEO, British Dyslexia Association

Preface

There is nothing unusual about being dyslexic or dyspraxic. About 1 in 20 people are dyslexic. About 1 in 20 are dyspraxic. However, in spite of these numbers, relatively few books have been written for adult dyslexics and dyspraxics that explore and explain in everyday language their lived experiences.

This book provides a non-academic explanation of why the everyday experiences of dyslexics and dyspraxics are different from those of other people in a number of crucial ways. It was written for more than just dyslexic and dyspraxic adults and those in their late teens. As so many dyslexics and dyspraxics have pointed out to me, they also want members of their own family and close friends to gain a better insight into why they do certain things, and why they think in different ways.

Many dyslexics and dyspraxics also pointed out to me that they want people they work with and work for, whether that be colleagues, employers, teachers or lecturers, to also understand them. All too frequently dyslexics and dyspraxics are misunderstood, and have been for far too long. This book is about dispelling myths and breaking down barriers of misunderstanding. It is written for non-professionals and professionals who want a clear insight into understanding the everyday lived experiences of being dyslexic and being dyspraxic. This understanding is the key to unleashing talent and hidden potential.

Acknowledgements

This book could not have been written without over 1,500 dyslexics and dyspraxics sharing with me their thoughts and experiences. To everyone, a big thank-you.

My family have also made a major contribution. My wife, Cathy, has helped me make my writing more succinct, questioned me on sections she did not understand, and improved my grammar. It is a better-written book because of her input. My eldest son, Matthew, has patiently year after year inputted data into a database and carried out statistical analyses. As a Genetics student he has also cast a critical eye over my observations and tracked down key papers. My youngest son, Daniel, is both dyslexic and has been Middlesex 800m County Champion in his age group for three successive years. Hence my particular interest in the links between sporting ability and dyslexia. I am very grateful for their input.

Hannah Evelyn French, an illustrator, graduated from Kingston University in 2003. I have always been impressed by how well, even as an undergraduate, she captured a range of dyslexic experiences in her work. As a dyslexic herself she could immediately understand what I was looking for whenever I asked her for an illustration.

Thanks are due to Tanya Watkins, fashion designer, for permission to use illustrations taken from her undergraduate portfolio. Tanya graduated in Fashion from Kingston University with a first-class degree.

Acknowledgements

At a time when dyspraxia was almost unknown in higher education, David Laycock, CBE, and Head of the Computer Centre for People with Disabilities, University of Westminster, was very supportive of my early concerns that dyspraxic students were being both misdiagnosed and overlooked. His full support was very important, so thank you.

I am also grateful for the feedback from many university and college staff who encouraged me in my belief that there is still much of importance to be said about dyslexia and dyspraxia.

Introduction

Dyslexia is far more than just a label – it is a lifestyle. As a label it is associated with many different meanings and emotions. For some people being told they are dyslexic is a moment of liberation: 'I was so anxious you were going to tell me I was thick. Knowing I'm dyslexic is the best day of my life.'

For others, being told they are dyslexic is a surprise: 'I thought dyslexia was all about writing letters backwards. I don't do that so I thought I couldn't be dyslexic.'

This book is about both liberation and surprises. It is about liberation in the sense that even many people who know they are dyslexic don't fully understand what being a dyslexic is. It sets out to help develop and deepen personal understanding. This book is also about surprises, for there are many myths and misconceptions about dyslexia, and these are explored.

Issues of dyspraxia as well as dyslexia are also discussed. Although they may at first sight appear quite different conditions, they have many features in common and this overlap is much more extensive than many people realise. In addition, it is quite common to find signs of dyspraxia when dyslexia is present, and signs of dyslexia when dyspraxia is the first diagnosis.

This book is also about the individuality of people who are dyslexic or dyspraxic. The labels 'dyslexia' and 'dyspraxia' are misleading for they suggest that everyone who is dyslexic or dyspraxic is exactly the same. I prefer the terms 'dyslexias' and 'dyspraxias' because they help to break away from this misleading stereotyping.

I would also argue that being dyslexic or dyspraxic should be considered as a lifestyle – dyslexia is not just about difficulties with reading and spelling, and dyspraxia is not just about clumsiness or difficulties with pronunciation. Being dyslexic and dyspraxic means that your everyday life is influenced and shaped in a variety of different ways. This book explores those everyday experiences.

This book is purposely written in an informal style. The reason for this is simple – I have read too many books about dyslexia which are dyslexia-unfriendly as they are too academic. I wanted to write something that most dyslexic and dyspraxic students would feel reasonably comfortable with. Secondly, many of the dyslexics and dyspraxics I have met find it difficult to explain to others what being dyslexic or dyspraxic is like since they are themselves unsure which of their experiences are due to dyslexia or dyspraxia and which are not. I therefore wanted to write a book that their parents, partners and siblings could also read and learn from. I have chosen to illustrate the ideas and concepts by using the actual words of dyslexics and dyspraxics I have met, for it is they who are living the experience of being dyslexic and dyspraxic.

In order to learn, you have to listen. Many years ago Ewan MacColl, a great songwriter, explained how he learnt from listening. He pointed out that when people are first asked questions about their lives, they spend about the first 20 minutes telling you what they think you want to know. After that they tell you about themselves. By listening, it became very evident to me that being dyslexic or being dyspraxic is a lived experience that influences so many aspects of everyday life.

Over the past six years I have listened to over 1,500 dyslexics and dyspraxics talking and discussing their personal histories and everyday experiences. Mainly students in higher education, they ranged in age from 17 to 61. In spite of this collective wealth of experience, and very impressive levels of intellectual ability, the thing that struck me most was how little is known and understood about dyslexia and dyspraxia.

When you ask questions about dyslexia most people immediately think of some kind of difficulties with reading. It is not obvious that going into a room to collect something, only to find you have forgotten what you went for, might also be related to being dyslexic. It is even less obvious that using the time before drifting off to sleep to sort through the day's events and plan for the following day is also a frequent dyslexic and dyspraxic experience. By creating space to listen, so much can be learnt.

Through listening carefully to detailed personal histories, I gradually developed a much wider range of questions to draw upon when assessing whether someone is dyslexic or dyspraxic. This took me into unexplored areas. However, it is one thing to ask questions, but another matter to bring the answers together and draw inferences. For this reason I had a database constructed and for the past five years I have explored the data on an annual basis. It is very easy to overlook something of potential interest if it only occurs occasionally. However, by being systematic, details can be captured that might otherwise escape attention.

When an interesting trend emerges it is vital to explore whether it is repeated in subsequent years. This is important in that a pattern based on a small number is always suspect. For example, in any one year I might encounter 25 out of 200+ students who have represented their county or country at sports.

However, when this type of figure occurs year after year, the evidence builds up. So when I make the statement that about 13% of the dyslexic students I have seen have represented their county/country in a sporting activity, or that the incidence of birth complications is very low for these students, these statements are based on consistent observations over more than three years.

The definition of a scientist as being someone who sees the same things as others but thinks about them differently is one that appeals to me. In one sense, virtually all the observations I have made could have been made 50 years ago – However, it does help to have an electronic database. The thinking differently is another matter.

In writing this book I wanted to move beyond pure descriptions to also come up with possible explanations. This, at times, inevitably requires speculative thinking. Unlike most psychologists who study and research dyslexia and dyspraxia, I had the advantage of not being wedded to one specific theory or hypothesis about underlying causes. I could stand back. I also know, from having taught about creativity and innovation for some years, that new ideas often emerge from finding solutions to questions outside of the immediate field being studied. Standing back provides that space to think outside of the box. Consequently, the research literature I have consulted is unusually wide – taking in genetics, the life histories of creative achievers and cognitive neuropsychology.

Most of this research is published in academic journals and is written in a very complex and dense style, as it is aimed at researchers rather than the lay public. While I have drawn upon this research to inform my ideas and observations, I have avoided citing endless names and dates when writing each chapter. As it was my intention to keep the style of writing as informal as possible, I have not included copious citations. My thinking has been informed by many different researchers and writers, but I would like to think it has also been inspired and shaped by the *agent provocateur* spirit of such great psychologists as Norman Geschwind.

Thinking 'outside of the box' is an exciting adventure. You may not always be right but sometimes you can point ideas in a different direction. I sense that most research into dyslexia and dyspraxia has somehow missed the person who is experiencing it. This book, for me, is an attempt to get back to the person. I hope it works for you.

Chapter 1

Dyslexia and Dyspraxia – The Common Ground

Most books about dyslexia start off by focusing on reading and spelling. Most books about dyspraxia begin by discussing problems with co-ordination. These are important issues. They are not, however, the only issues. There are more common links between dyslexia and dyspraxia than distinguishing features. That is why this book breaks with tradition by initially describing and discussing similarities rather than differences. This chapter focuses on those shared experiences – the common ground, as it were. For many dyslexics and dyspraxics it is these experiences that colour and shape their everyday lives the most. They are also often the most noticeable features.

Many of the students I see tell me how disorganised they are. In addition, they very often describe themselves as having a poor memory and poor concentration. Consequently they are likely to misplace things, forget what they were going to say halfway through a sentence, miss appointments and make use of sticky notes and lists. They are also easily distracted and experience difficulties when copying notes down from an overhead projector as they find it hard to remember more than three or four words at a time.

All of these experiences, as well as many others, are the result of a weak working memory. This statement needs to be explained, for there are different types of memory, and two types of working memory. I am using the term 'working memory' to refer very specifically to a short-term memory for verbal information. For example, imagine you are new to a college or university and you ask someone how to get to the students' union from where you are. When you are told, 'Go straight to the end of the corridor, turn left, and it's the third door on the right', you have to use your working memory to retain this information while you walk towards the students' union.

This type of working memory refers to a memory store that enables you to actively organise and think about verbal information for a short time. The term 'working memory' is a better one than 'short-term memory' for it captures the manner in which we think consciously about things. A key feature about working memory is that it is of limited capacity. Some people have a greater capacity than others.

In general, working memory capacity is linked to level of verbal reasoning. A high verbal ability is accompanied by an above average working memory capacity. A low level of verbal ability is usually accompanied by a smaller working memory capacity. This harmony of linkage is not observed in most instances of dyslexia or dyspraxia. As a fairly broad generalisation, the working memory space that is available for someone who is dyslexic or dyspraxic is less than they need for their level of ability. In many cases it is much less. In addition, working memory also appears to be more fragile.

The impact of limited working memory capacity

A lack of working memory capacity affects both academic life and everyday social and working life. For example, to take good notes in a lecture requires doing a number of different things at the same time. First, you need to be able to follow the theme of the lecture in order to understand the points that are being made. Second, you have to be able to identify what is important so you can make a note of the main points. That is, you have to know how to be selective. Third, you also need to be able to write down what is important. All these activities require the use of working memory space. On top of all this you have to be able to write quickly and spell well.

Taking good notes can be difficult even for someone who is not dyslexic or dyspraxic. For a dyslexic or dyspraxic person, note-taking is even more difficult because working memory space becomes overwhelmed very quickly, so some elements get squeezed out. As a consequence, doing more than one thing at a time becomes almost impossible when working memory is weak. For example, in a lecture some students just listen to make sure they have understood what is being said. Others try to take notes without really understanding what is being said. This is why being allowed to make a recording of a lecture is so important. It is also very helpful if a lecturer provides good-quality lecture notes, preferably in advance.

A weak working memory also affects the copying of information. Most lecturers make use of either an overhead projector or PowerPoint presentations. Poor reading skills obviously slow down the rate at which information can be read. However, a weak working memory also slows down the rate at which information can be copied.

If you are non-dyslexic, you can probably read through the following sentence and remember all of it while you write it down: 'Sperry was awarded the Nobel prize for his pioneering work in the 1930s on neuronal regeneration.' Being dyslexic or dyspraxic will probably result in you remembering only a small part of the sentence while you are writing it down. Consequently, you have to spend more time looking from the text to your notes and back again when copying information down. You also have to scan to find your place again each time you go back to the text. Copying information down therefore takes considerably longer. If you also have to stop and think 'How do I spell "pioneering"? How do I spell, "neuronal"?', it can feel as if it is taking forever to copy the information. While you are concentrating on remembering what it is you have to copy, there is no spare capacity to take in what the lecturer is saying.

Hannah's illustration captures her own experience of being in a lecture. It is as if she is being so swamped by the words of the lecturer that she is no longer able to take in what is being said.

It is not surprising that most dyslexic and dyspraxic children and teenagers find so many school lessons so frustrating. If a teacher starts off the lesson by saying, 'I want you do this, and then this, and when you have finished these make a start on this page of this exercise', by the time the teacher has reached the end of the list of things to do you will have forgotten what the first task was. You might then ask your friend what you have to do and this may be misinterpreted by the teacher as you not paying attention or being disruptive.

In one or two subjects, such as maths, the difficulty with remembering more than a few things at a time makes it particularly hard to remember all the steps of a sequence that is being worked through. However, a weak working memory does not necessarily mean you will be poor at maths – I have seen some brilliant dyslexic and dyspraxic mathematicians. One captured the impact of his weak working memory quite succinctly: 'I find the easy maths difficult, and the difficult maths easy.' By 'easy maths' he was referring to learning the times tables and doing mental arithmetic. By 'difficult maths' he was referring to concepts such as matrices and calculus.

Because a weak working memory often results in very noticeable difficulties with the learning of basic arithmetical processes such as multiplication and division, there is a danger that these difficulties will result in the suggestion that dyscalculia (a specific difficulty with numbers) is present. In my experience, dyscalculia, which in its pure form is a fundamental difficulty with the concepts of 'greater than' and 'less than', is very rare.

A weak working memory also affects the writing of essays. Many students tell me that they find starting to write an essay 'the worst part'. This is not surprising. Writing an essay or report is like creating a complex story with lots of characters. As the writer, you have to decide what the story-line is and the order of appearance of the characters. To plan and tell the story well requires lots of working memory capacity.

Limited working memory capacity makes it impossible to think about all aspects of the story at once, because it imposes a limit on the number of ideas that can be actively considered at the same time. This results in the realisation that 'it's not going to work' and another attempt is made to think of how to organise all the ideas. And then another, and another, until frustration sets in and you go off to make a cup of tea or coffee instead. One student spoke for many when he referred to his difficulties with starting an essay as being 'the white sheet syndrome'.

For many students, trying to work out how to start writing an essay is akin to looking at their ideas through a kaleidoscope. Each time they think about what to do, the picture changes. The problem is that a limited working memory means that only part of the picture can be thought of at any one time, rather than the whole picture. It is therefore not surprising that the writing of an essay gets repeatedly put off until the last possible minute.

Fortunately, there are ways of getting around these memory limitations. For many dyslexic and dyspraxic students, but not all, visual memory is much better than working memory. This means that mind-maps and spider-diagrams can be very useful. If these are drawn by hand they can get quite messy and this is why a software program such as Inspiration can be so important. (See the Appendix for details of where to purchase specialist software.) By being able to drag ideas around on the screen and change text, the visual scheme of ideas can be kept very clean. The use of colour-coding and icons also makes it possible to group ideas together so links can be seen easily.

The difficulty with arranging ideas to arrive at an essay that has a good internal logic and structure means that many dyslexics and dyspraxics often have to rewrite an essay a number of times. It is not uncommon to be told, 'It takes me three times as long as anyone else.' Even making notes from books at the research stage for an essay can be problematic. Making notes requires an ability to select what is important. This involves being able to think about a number of ideas simultaneously so that only the most appropriate elements are selected.

A weak working memory also affects the structuring of sentences. Many dyslexics and dyspraxics have a tendency to write very long sentences that ramble. When memory is limited the whole of that working space might be taken up with just one phrase, which then sparks the next idea, and then the next, and so on. Consequently, punctuation and internal logic suffer. Also, the completed 'sentence' will contain too many ideas and will often go off at a tangent.

Sometimes, the writing of a sentence will come to a complete halt due to stopping to think about a spelling. Because sorting this out can occupy all of the working memory capacity, the original idea that was in the process of being written down ends up being forgotten. Students tell me that when this happens they have to reread what they have just written in order to work out what they were going to say next. It is not surprising that so many students say they find it very hard to express their ideas in writing: 'I know it in my head but I can't get it down on paper.'

A weak working memory doesn't just have an impact on taking notes and writing essays; it affects everyday life as well. A high proportion of dyslexic and dyspraxic students describe themselves as being disorganised, a 'bit dippy'. They give as examples forgetting appointments, misplacing items, not returning books on time, and going to a room to fetch something only to find they have forgotten what they went for. Because forgetfulness is such a general problem, different people develop different coping strategies.

Some people have everything strewn around their room. Although this may appear to be disorganised, sometimes – and I stress the 'sometimes' – it can be a deliberate way of arranging things because everything is on display, and visual memory can be used to remember where particular items are.

Some students use their mobile phones as personal organisers and also text themselves messages of things they need to remember. Others use sticky notes and diaries. It is not unusual for someone with a weak working memory to write themselves a note on the back of their hand.

Some students pack everything they need for the next morning the night before, to ensure things don't get forgotten when they leave the house the following morning. Others develop a routine of patting themselves – 'Have I got my wallet/watch/mobile/keys?' – before going out of the house or leaving a pub.

A weak working memory is, in my experience, observed in over 90% of students who are dyslexic or dyspraxic. However, in a very small minority, more so in instances of dyspraxia than dyslexia, working memory capacity is fine. As always, it is misleading to take a broad generalisation and apply it in all cases.

The fragility of working memory

Many students have told me how, during a conversation, ideas often occur to them suddenly and they go off at a tangent. On other occasions, they will be about to say something, only to realise they have forgotten what they wanted to say. Most students tell me how easily they can lose concentration – 'My mind wanders very easily' – and how they were told off at school for daydreaming. These are all examples of the fragility of working memory.

In one sense working memory has to be fragile in that new information is constantly replacing current information. However, the manner in which information is replaced appears to be much more of a random process for dyslexics and dyspraxics than for non-dyslexic and non-dyspraxic people. I suspect that two factors may be responsible for this fragility: limited memory capacity and an inefficient executive function.

Limited memory capacity implies an imbalance between working memory capacity and verbal reasoning abilities. When a full psychological assessment is carried out using what is commonly known as the WAIS (Wechsler Adult Intelligence Scales), now in its third edition, or WISC (Wechsler Intelligence Scales for Children), now in its fourth edition, both working memory and verbal reasoning are measured. Ideally, these abilities should be in equilibrium. If, however, working memory capacity is much lower than the level required to be in balance with verbal reasoning, then a working memory deficit is formally recorded.

It is important to note that working memory capacity does not have to be below average for a weak working memory to be recorded. I have seen a number of bright students who have scored higher on working memory than the average person. However, for these students there is still a significant gap between their scores for working memory and verbal reasoning.

When this imbalance occurs it is as if the brain is generating more ideas than can be accommodated within the available working memory space. This results in a log-jam of ideas building up outside of working memory. Consequently, it is as if these ideas jostle competitively to gain access to the working memory space.

Access to working memory is controlled by what psychologists call the executive function. This does a number of things, such as prioritising what information gains entry to working memory space and controlling the direction of attention. Without such a mechanism our conscious experience of working memory would be one of total chaos.

An analogy to illustrate this is to think of the executive function as being a bouncer outside a select nightclub – the more limited the working memory, the more select the nightclub. There is therefore great competition to gain entrance to this nightclub. When the nightclub is full, the only way someone can gain entry is when someone else leaves. The greater the crowd outside, the more difficulties the bouncer will have, and the more chance there is of someone gatecrashing and getting past the bouncer without permission.

In the case of someone with a weak working memory the executive function is not particularly effective, with the consequence that ideas occur suddenly without warning. As they burst into working memory, they create space by pushing an existing idea out of conscious thought. One student described this experience as feeling as if her ideas were being 'pushed over the edge'. Because ideas can come and go without warning, the conscious thought experience of many dyslexic and dyspraxic students is characterised by a sense of chaos and transience of ideas.

This experience was summed up well by one dyslexic Radio Broadcasting student I met. He described how, one evening in the students' union bar, an idea suddenly occurred to him, an idea he thought was brilliant.

'Quick,' he said to his friend, 'write this idea down and phone me in the morning to tell me what it is.' He was well aware that if he didn't capture his creative idea there and then, he would very quickly forget what it was. Sometimes thoughts can appear and disappear so rapidly they are like shooting stars, flashing across the conscious space of the mind. No sooner has an idea occurred than it vanishes.

I sometimes describe this experience of ideas coming out of nowhere and then disappearing just as quickly, as being a kind of 'Richard Branson' phenomenon. Richard Branson is dyslexic and his Virgin company is very different from most other commercial organisations. Most companies have a core business, such as making a specific kind of product or selling a specific service.

In contrast, the Virgin organisation is very different. It is essentially a brand name, a very well-known one that encompasses a diversity of activities, from financial services to drinks and travel. It is as if random ideas crash into Richard Branson's mind and grab his attention. He is, of course, skilled enough to discard ideas that won't work.

This fragility of thought appears to apply mainly to verbal thought. Visual thought seems to be more stable. For example, many dyslexic and dyspraxic students find they are very easily distracted when engaged in activities such as reading or writing. Although it could be argued that this is because they are not very interested in these activities, the same distractibility and unpredictability can also occur in conversation as well. One student told me, 'When an idea pops into my mind I have to say it straight away; otherwise I will forget it.' Many students describe going off at tangents during a conversation.

However, if engaged in a visual activity such as video editing, painting or drawing, or one with a high visual content such as playing hockey, football or sailing, then concentration can be intense and sustained, often for hours at a time. A key reason for this is that visual memory and thought take over and, in most cases, the visual memory capacity is considerably greater.

Many students have told me they have a very good memory for faces but are very poor at remembering names. Several art students have described how they try to overcome their poor memory for names by making sketches of the other students in their year and then writing the name of each student alongside the relevant sketch.

Most people, whether dyslexic or not, are better at remembering faces than names. It is just that, when working memory is poor, the difficulty with remembering names becomes much more obvious.

Processing speed

At the beginning of this chapter it was mentioned that a common link between dyslexia and dyspraxia is a weak working memory. A second common link is a slow speed of processing. Once again, this does not apply in all cases. However, it occurs with sufficient frequency to be recognised as an important feature that is often reported for both dyslexia and dyspraxia.

In carrying out a psychological assessment using the WAIS-III, four general sets of abilities are assessed and their levels calculated (for example, see Grant 2002). Two of these have already been mentioned – working memory and verbal reasoning (usually called Verbal

Comprehension). The other two sets of abilities are Processing Speed and Perceptual Organisation (visual reasoning). Processing Speed is assessed by how well an individual does on two tasks, both of which are visual in nature and require an ability to take in and search for simple visual symbols very quickly.

Although these two tasks involve a lower level of thinking than the three visual reasoning tasks that are used to determine a Perceptual Organisation score, they are important because they provide an indication of the speed at which simple or routine information can be processed and learnt without errors being made.

Ideally, the levels of Processing Speed and Perceptual Organisation should be in balance. For many dyslexics and dyspraxics this is not the case: Processing Speed is often well below the level recorded for Perceptual Organisation. This difference will affect a wide range of activities, including speed of reading, writing and drawing, ability to proofread well, and the types of sports and computer games that are preferred.

A typical WAIS profile for a dyslexic or dyspraxic student is shown below.

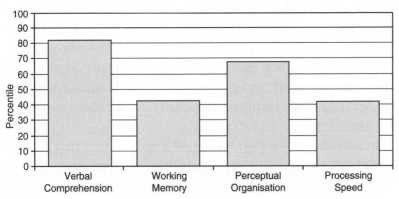

Figure 1.1 A typical dyslexic and dyspraxic WAIS-III profile expressed as percentile scores

This profile reveals very clearly that, for about 70% to 80% of dyslexic and dyspraxic students, scores for verbal and visual reasoning are much higher than scores for Working Memory and Processing Speed. (If there were no specific learning difficulties, such as dyslexia or dyspraxia, the WAIS profile would look fairly flat; that is, all four columns would be approximately the same height.)

The characteristic dyslexic and dyspraxic double spike profile occurs independently of age. When dyslexia or dyspraxia is present, it does not matter whether someone is 8, 18 or 68, the same profile is observed in about 80% of instances. You do not grow out of being dyslexic or dyspraxic even when special teaching improves reading skills or physiotherapy results in an improvement in motor co-ordination.

One way of interpreting this spiky profile is to think of the brain as a computer. Verbal Comprehension is akin to being the word processing software, while Working Memory is RAM (Random Access Memory). Perceptual Organisation can be thought of as the graphics card, and Processing Speed as the processing chip.

For many dyslexics and dyspraxics, it is as if they have a good-quality word processing package and graphics card, but limited memory and a slow processing chip. However, what it is not possible to do is go to the nearest computing store and buy additional memory and a faster chip. Instead, it is a question of learning how to get around the limitations so that full potential is achieved.

When processing speed is slow, a number of activities are affected. For example, many students have told me that when they are writing they often feel as if their brain is thinking faster than their hand can move. Because of this, it is as if, at times, their hand jumps to keep up so parts of words or even whole words may be left out. When proofreading, it is, as one student put it, 'as if my brain is ten words ahead of my eyes'. This is one key reason why proofreading is so difficult. In fact, it can be so challenging that a number of students give up on it.

TextHELP is a software package that can read aloud text displayed on a computer screen. This can be a great help in proofreading, for you can listen to what you have written and check that it sounds right. Dragon Naturally Speaking is a software package that converts speech to text. This takes away the slowness of writing and difficulties with spelling. It is also now a very powerful piece of software and it can learn to recognise most voices – but not all – within ten minutes (although it takes much longer to learn the commands).

A slow speed of processing will also affect reading. Reading requires doing many things simultaneously – you have to scan lines of visual symbols and discriminate very quickly between shapes, be able to understand what you are reading, as well as remember what you have just read.

Whereas many dyslexics and dyspraxics are good at the verbal thinking requirements, if the processing is slow and working memory weak, the ability to understand and think about what has been just read will be disrupted. When there is an imbalance between speed of processing and speed of thought, it is not surprising that words get misread. It is as if part of the brain wants to go faster than it is receiving information and it starts to make guesses at what a word might be.

A slow speed of processing also affects activities that require fast responses, such as some sports and computer games. One student who had reached the semi-professional level in football was puzzled why, even though he practised each day for hours at a time, he was always a fraction of a second off the pace. However, because of his excellent visual reasoning abilities, he could 'read' a game very well and was particularly good at defending. Once he had viewed his profile he immediately understood his strengths and weaknesses.

Very few people reach a semi-professional level in sports. Many more people play computer games. In many cases, people with a much higher visual reasoning ability than processing speed prefer to play games of strategy rather than ones that depend purely on speed of response. This slowness of response can also be seen when scrolling through text on a computer monitor. If speed of processing is slow, rapid scrolling is very difficult even when reading skills are good.

Even activities such as crossing a busy road on foot, driving in traffic or walking along a crowded pavement can become slightly more difficult if processing speed is slow. When a slow processing speed is also accompanied by a weak short-term visual memory (this combination occurs in about 10% of people), these types of everyday activities become even more challenging. A slow processing speed may also influence styles of drawing. This particular aspect will be discussed in Chapter 5.

A slow speed of processing, in combination with a weak working memory, results in many dyslexics and dyspraxics disliking being asked to work under pressure. A number of students have told me that, provided they are left to work by themselves, they can achieve a high standard. But this has to be without pressure.

To summarise what has been covered so far: a weak working memory and a slow speed of processing are typical aspects of being dyslexic and dyspraxic. They are not, however, causes of dyslexia or dyspraxia. Each factor influences a surprisingly wide variety of everyday experiences at home, work and college or university. Because of this it is appropriate to think of being dyslexic or dyspraxic as a particular kind of lifestyle.

The next two chapters will focus on the need to think about the different forms that the dyslexias and dyspraxias can take.

Chapter 2

What is Dyslexia?

Most definitions of dyslexia are too narrow, tending to focus on difficulties with learning to read. In reality dyslexia is extremely complex. This chapter will begin with the simplistic view and go on to describe and discuss the complexity that the dyslexias are.

Central to most definitions of dyslexia is the requirement that reading ability is unexpectedly poor and that there is no adequate explanation to account for this other than dyslexia. As will be explained later, this is a narrow view of what dyslexia is in reality. However, in practice, this requirement has to be satisfied to arrive at a diagnosis of dyslexia and this is the starting point for considering its complexity.

The only satisfactory way to determine whether reading skills are unexpectedly poor is to measure and compare an individual's level of intellectual ability with their level of reading performance. (Spelling ability is usually assessed at the same time as well.) A personal history is also required, for if a difference is recorded the personal history will then help determine whether the difference is genuinely an unexpected one.

The question of which intellectual abilities to measure is crucial, since not all measures are suitable. In my view it is important to compare like with like. For this reason I place the greatest importance on the comparison of reading (and spelling) skills with verbal reasoning skills. Most diagnostic tests of verbal reasoning ability are carried out orally and measure knowledge and understanding of language through asking questions about the meanings of words and relationships between words.

Questions about the meanings of words typically take the form of 'Can you explain the meaning of the word "adolescent"?' Relationships between words are explored by asking questions such as 'In what ways are "drizzle" and "monsoon" similar to each other?' These questions are explored orally so that there are no reading or writing requirements. The questions are presented in sequence, going from quite simple questions to very hard ones. For example, most people can explain what a mountain is. It is much harder to explain the meaning of the word 'paradigm'. As you would expect, some people are better at these kinds of tasks than others, but that is not important. What is important is how the score for an individual compares with that person's own scores for reading and spelling.

In general, the relationship between measures of verbal reasoning and reading and spelling abilities is an approximate one. That is, while there is a strong tendency for them to be roughly equal, some variation is to be expected. Nevertheless, for some people, the extent of the variation can be surprisingly great.

Jane is typical of many dyslexic students I see. While her verbal reasoning performance places her in the top 20% of the population, her word reading accuracy score puts her in the bottom 10%. This is an unexpected difference given Jane's much higher level of verbal reasoning. If dyslexia were not present, her skills of reading and spelling would be at least average, and probably above.

There will probably always be debate about how big the gap has to be between levels of reading skills and verbal comprehension before dyslexia can be said to be present, but virtually all diagnoses of dyslexia are dependent on demonstrating an unexpected difference. Usually, if reading skills are weak, spelling is also weak. However, some people have very good reading skills but are very weak at spelling. Although it is a term not often used in the UK, the word 'dysorthographic' describes a person who has an unexpected weakness purely in spelling.

In order to demonstrate that a discrepancy between reading (and spelling) and verbal reasoning is an unexpected one, it is necessary to know key details about a person's life. For example, one student, Shona, had been brought up in a country where even primary school children had to pay to be educated. Her family was very poor and her primary and secondary education totalled just eighteen months. Not unexpectedly, her skills of reading and spelling were below average, but by only a little. Shona's verbal reasoning skills were a little above average. Given the circumstance, her skills of reading and spelling were very much better than might have been expected. Shona was not dyslexic. Her history also demonstrated how quickly some people can learn to read and spell.

When comparing reading and spelling abilities with intellectual abilities I have stressed the need to use verbal reasoning skills as the basis for comparison. I'll explain why that is important. The most commonly used measures of intellectual ability in a diagnostic setting are the Wechsler Intelligence Scales (see Chapter 1). There is a version for children and young teenagers

(WISC) and a version for adults (WAIS). Each version consists of a series of subtests which are used to measure performance on a range of different skills, including knowledge of vocabulary, mental arithmetic, three-dimensional thinking and speed of copying symbols. When all the scores are combined, IQ can be calculated.

For someone who is dyslexic it is unwise to use an IQ figure as a point of comparison with reading and spelling. This is because, in virtually all cases of dyslexia, an IQ measure would hide very important variations such as just how good – or poor – someone is at certain kinds of activities. In most cases a typical dyslexic Wechsler profile reveals higher scores for verbal and visual reasoning than for short-term memory and speed of visual processing. When no specific learning difficulties are present the Wechsler profile will be fairly flat, not spiky.

Jane's spiky profile (see Figure 2.1) is typical of a dyslexic student in that she scored above average on verbal and visual reasoning (Perceptual Organisation) skills and below average on Working Memory and Processing Speed. Whereas her Verbal Comprehension (verbal reasoning) and Perceptual Organisation (visual

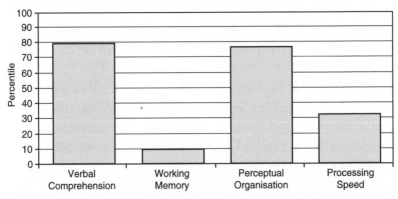

Figure 2.1 Jane's WAIS-III profile expressed as percentile scores

reasoning) scores put her in the top 20% and top 23% of the population respectively, her scores for Working Memory and Processing Speed put her in the bottom 9% and 32% respectively.

This type of variation is important as it helps to explain a number of everyday experiences (see Chapter 1). However, once these scores are combined, the variation is lost and a false picture emerges. If Jane's Verbal IQ is calculated by combining her verbal reasoning and working memory scores, her Verbal IQ score places her in the bottom 45% of the population. This is a big drop from being in the top 20% for verbal reasoning.

The same kind of thing happens if scores from the subtests of visual reasoning and processing speed are combined to calculate Jane's Performance IQ. Whereas Jane's score for visual reasoning places her in the top 23% of the population, her Performance IQ pushes her down to the top 37%. Finally, when Verbal IQ and Performance IQ are together used to calculate a general IQ score, Jane's IQ of 101 places her just above the midpoint of 100 for the population. As she is actually of 'high average' ability on tests of verbal and visual reasoning, her IQ score is not a fair reflection of her real abilities, nor does it reveal the barriers that prevent her from achieving her full potential.

Whereas Jane's level of verbal reasoning places her in the top 20% of the population, her levels of reading and spelling put her in the bottom 10% and 8% respectively, differences of 70 and 72 percentile points. These are major discrepancies. However, if you just compare her reading with her IQ, the discrepancy will be much smaller – just 40 percentile points.

It is important to note that it is the extent of the discrepancy between the scores for reading and verbal reasoning that is the key to arriving at a diagnosis of dyslexia, not the level of reading by itself. That is, it is not necessary to be really poor at reading to be diagnosed as being dyslexic. While I have met several students whose reading skills are so poor that they find travelling difficult because they cannot read the names of stations or roads, most students I see can read. Probably about 10% choose to read for pleasure.

It is not true that dyslexics cannot read. Most can, but their reading ability is well below expectation. For example, I frequently see students whose performance on the assessment of verbal reasoning places them in the top 1% of the population. However, their reading puts them in the bottom 30% or 40% of the population. While it is the case that these students can read some types of books and newspapers with a fair degree of accuracy and fluency, their real reading difficulties only become apparent when reading academic books and research papers.

One student described how, when reading a novel, she just 'flowed with the story' and skipped over words she didn't recognise. However, when reading an academic text, she has to read every word and concentrate on remembering what she has just read. Reading is not just a question of reading words with accuracy. It is also being able to retain the information and not be distracted while reading, both of which are well-known dyslexic features. Hannah's illustration of herself 'reading' but not taking in what she is reading captures this typical dyslexic challenge. On top of this, Meares-Irlen Syndrome may also be present (see Chapter 4). It is important to remember that reading is a multi-skilled process.

Because the profile of abilities for dyslexics is an uneven one, some definitions of dyslexia state that, in

addition to an unexpected weakness in reading and spelling, dyslexia is characterised by one or more cognitive weaknesses as well. (The word 'cognitive' just means a mental process carried out by the brain, such as remembering.) This is the definition I favour, as it helps to focus attention on the complex nature of dyslexia.

You will notice that this definition does not state which cognitive weakness, or weaknesses, have to be present. This is important, for the reality of dyslexia is that there are a variety of dyslexias, not just one. One of the most influential books on dyslexia was written more than 60 years ago, by the English educational psychologist Fred Schonell. Schonell did not use the term 'dyslexia' as it was not in common use at that time, but instead referred to 'backward readers and spellers'. In his 1945 book he describes three different patterns of reading difficulties. He points out that some children, who he called auditorily weak, have very good visual recognition skills but poor phonological skills. Others have the reverse profile. That is, visually weak children have good phonological skills but are poor at visual recognition. Yet others are poor at both phonological processing and visual recognition.

This type of differentiation is important in that good phonological and visual skills are necessary to read well in English. This is because English contains many irregular words that are not spelt as they sound and so do not follow the general phonetic spelling rules. When words are regular they are easy to read and to pronounce correctly, even if you have never encountered them before.

For example, if you have good phonological skills you will be able to read the sentence 'Zog norded nov Mungent' with some fluency and accuracy as each nonsense word is a regularly spelt word. However, when a word is irregular, it has to be recognised from its shape. For example, the sentence 'The reigning sovereign campaigned from her yacht' contains four irregular words. Those dyslexics with good visual recognition skills but poor phonological ones would be able to read 'The reigning sovereign campaigned from her yacht' with little difficulty, but would really struggle with 'Zog norded nov Mungent'.

Unlike English, a number of languages such as Italian and Spanish (but not Hispanic Spanish) are phonetically regular. A visually weak dyslexic Italian or Spanish person would not necessarily encounter major difficulties with learning to read or write in their own language. However, it is highly likely that the process of learning will be slow, for the other facets of dyslexia would still apply, such as finding it hard to remember what they have just read, and daydreaming at school when they should be reading or listening to the teacher.

Maria is a classic example of a visually weak Spanish dyslexic. Her teachers and parents could never understand why she always performed badly in exams and assignments at school when she had a very good vocabulary and her verbal skills were excellent. Reading in Spanish was not a problem for Maria and, when she lived at home, she read three to four books a month for pleasure. Maria had to learn English at school, but because she found it so difficult her parents paid for her to visit the UK to practise. When Maria was 14 she had still not learnt all the times tables, and her parents paid for her to have private maths tuition. She also had to repeat a year at high school. Her mother always complained about how disorganised Maria was.

Maria eventually enrolled, as a mature student, at an art college in the UK, which provided the opportunity for her to be assessed. This assessment revealed an excellent level of verbal comprehension but a very weak working memory. In addition, her short-term visual memory was also poor. (This means that when she looks at something and then looks away, her visual memory fades away much faster than would be expected.)

Maria can read regularly spelt English words with virtually no problems. However, her error rate for irregular English words is nine times greater than for regular ones. That is, her memory for the shape of words is very poor.

If we define dyslexia as being an unexpected difficulty with acquiring reading skills, Maria is dyslexic when assessed on her reading in English but not dyslexic when assessed on her Spanish reading skills. However, her cognitive profile remains the same whether she is living in Spain or the UK, and her everyday experiences and behaviours are typical of dyslexia. By knowing about the different forms that dyslexia can take, it is possible to understand why this is so. This is why it is so important to realise that dyslexia is more than just an unexpected difficulty with reading. The underlying cognitive landscape differs from dyslexic to dyslexic.

This individual complexity is captured in Ian Smythe's (2005) definition of dyslexia:

> Dyslexia is the specific difficulty with the acquisition of literacy skills (reading, writing and spelling) which may be caused by a combination of phonological, visual and auditory processing deficits. Word retrieval and speed of processing difficulties may also be present. The manifestation of dyslexia in any individual will depend upon not only individual cognitive differences, but also the language used.

It is more than 60 years since Schonell first described three different subtypes of dyslexia. Since then there have been several more attempts to identify differing forms of dyslexia. For example, Elena Boder (1973) in the USA, and Andrew Ellis (1984) in the UK, each advanced the case for there being three types of dyslexia, but with little general success. Interestingly, the match between the subtypes proposed by Schonell, Ellis and Boder is a very close one, and some researchers (eg. Ben-Yehudah *et al.* 2001), still take care to make use of these three general categories of dyslexia.

Probably the reason why Schonell, Ellis and Boder enjoyed little practical recognition when they subdivided dyslexia into three subtypes is that, in practice, it is not always clear-cut as to which category of dyslexia a person should be assigned to, and sometimes no category appears to be appropriate. This does not mean that we should therefore think of dyslexia as being a unitary concept. It is far more helpful to recognise that dyslexia is a combination of strengths and weaknesses, and that dyslexic profiles can often be quite different from each other in a number of ways, without having to worry about how many types of dyslexia there are. Nevertheless, it would be a major step forward if we spoke of 'the dyslexias', as this would at least draw attention to the need to think about the particular range of characteristics each individual has.

The advantage of using the Wechsler Intelligence Scales as part of a diagnostic assessment is that, by plotting out the four Index scores of Verbal Comprehension, Working Memory, Perceptual Organisation and Processing Speed, different profiles are revealed. Although Jane's double spike profile is the one most commonly found in assessments, there are significant variations from this. For example, Figure 2.2 reveals that Juliette's performance on visual reasoning (Perceptual Organisation) and processing speed is well above her verbal reasoning ability, but her score for Working Memory is particularly low. Whereas her Processing Speed score (her highest score) places her in the top 10% of the population, her Working Memory score puts her in the bottom 10%.

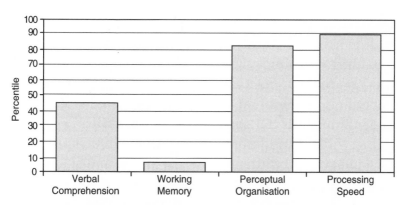

Figure 2.2 Juliette's four WAIS Index scores expressed as percentile scores

Jason's profile (see Figure 2.3) is almost a mirror image of Juliette's. His Working Memory score is above

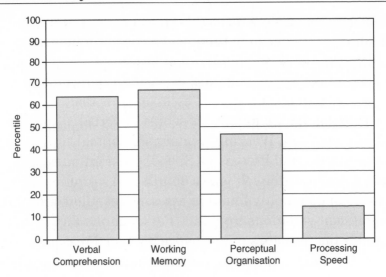

Figure 2.3   Jason's four WAIS Index scores expressed as
            percentile scores

average and on a par with his Verbal Comprehension
score. However, his Processing Speed score places him
in the bottom 14%. Interestingly, Jason's reading profile
revealed he made five times as many errors when
reading irregular words than regular ones, and his speed
of reading was almost half that expected of an
undergraduate. In many ways he is typical of the reader
that Schonell identified as having poor visual word
recognition skills but good phonological skills.

Jane, Juliette and Jason are all dyslexic in that all three
have unexpected difficulties with reading and spelling.
They all have one or more cognitive weaknesses as well
as strengths. However, their cognitive profiles are
significantly different and these differences will be
reflected in their everyday experiences. For example,
Juliette is inclined to be impulsive and very forgetful,
while Jason dislikes having to work under pressure and
prefers to think carefully about his responses before

answering questions. Because the factors underlying dyslexic cognitive profiles influence and colour such a wide range of everyday behaviours and experiences, it is more helpful to think of dyslexia as being a lifestyle – and a style that is for life.

Although the profile of a dyslexic person frequently reveals cognitive strengths and weaknesses, it is important to realise that these weaknesses are part of being dyslexic, but do not cause the dyslexia. The typical double spike observed for many dyslexics is often found in instances of dyspraxia as well (see Chapter 3), even when reading and spelling are good. Very occasionally, this double spike profile is observed when a person is neither dyslexic nor dyspraxic. In order to understand what dyslexia is, it is necessary to understand what lies beneath the profiles.

There has been no shortage of attempts to explain the basis of dyslexia. Currently there are four popular major theories. Rather than asking which one is right, I believe it is more helpful to think of them as providing different perspectives on what is a complex neurological picture.

The word 'dyslexia' literally means 'difficulties with language' and was first coined about 130 years ago. There has always been debate about whether dyslexia is just a difficulty with language or a mixture of verbal and visual components. Probably for the past 20 years the most popular theoretical explanation has been that dyslexia is the result of phonological processing difficulties.

The first name that comes to mind when this theory is mentioned is likely to be that of Professor Margaret Snowling. She claims that 'Dyslexia is a specific form of language impairment that affects the way the brain encodes the phonological features of spoken words. The core deficit is in phonological processing. . .' (Snowling 2000: 213). Phonological processing refers to the brain's ability to break down a stream of sounds into very small parts when listening to someone talk and then recombine the units to make sense of what is being said. If there is a weakness in phonological processing, this will have an impact on a range of experiences.

For example, some dyslexics find it hard to follow a conversation in a noisy environment even though others have no such difficulty. Some confuse similar-sounding words, such as 'specific' and 'Pacific'. This phonological weakness also affects the ability to match the right letters to sounds when spelling. For example, an attempt to spell 'quarrel' might result in 'corral'. It will also affect the ability to learn how to break words down into their component sounds when learning to read, as well as the ability to remember verbal information for a short period of time. It is as if the brain is trying to remember and recall auditory information that is not very clear or well-defined. This is why it can be difficult to hold information in working memory.

It may affect long-term memory as well, for information has to be both stored and retrieved with precision. If the auditory sounds are slightly fuzzy it will take slightly longer to retrieve the information. Often someone will say that they know the answer to a question, but can't quite arrive at it on demand. This is sometimes called the 'tip-of-the-tongue' phenomenon.

A few psychologists have gone so far as to recommend that dyslexia be defined just as a weakness in phonological processing. They point out that by adopting this approach there is no longer a need to assess intellectual abilities. However, most psychologists and educationalists are wary of going down this path. Jane's profile shows that there are two key cognitive weaknesses associated with dyslexia, not one. In my experience, this double spike profile is observed in about 80% of dyslexics I have seen.

However, Jason is one of the 20% of dyslexics without a double spike profile. His profile is important because it reveals that there are some dyslexic people who do not have a weak working memory. This poses a problem for those who argue that phonological processing is the defining feature of dyslexia.

Another problem for the phonologists, as will be revealed in the next chapter, is that some dyspraxics have excellent reading and spelling skills but still have a weak working memory. If a difficulty with phonological processing results in problems with learning to read and spell, as well as with working memory, how can someone be good at reading but poor at remembering things for a short period of time? These questions remain unanswered.

While the work of Margaret Snowling is important and has been very influential, the phonological deficit hypothesis is just one of several attempts to provide a causal explanation of the nature of dyslexia. Currently there are at least three other major theories offered as alternatives. The double deficit hypothesis that has been developed by Maryanne Wolf and her colleagues (for example, see Wolf and O'Brien 2001) states that, in addition to a phonological deficit, there is also a speed of processing deficit. This double deficit concept sits well with the double spike seen in most Wechsler profiles. However, as Juliette's profile reveals, not all dyslexics experience a problem with speed of timing. Once again, there are problems with trying to generalise about dyslexia.

Professor John Stein (for example see Stein *et al.* 2001) has developed quite a different theory – the magnocellular theory – to account for dyslexia. Central to this is the proposition that the brains of dyslexics have fewer magnocellular cells than those of non-dyslexics, especially in the pathway that conveys visual information from the eyes to the back of the brain and the specialised visual fields. The available evidence to date (such as Ramus *et al.* 2003) suggests that while this is probably true for some dyslexics, it does not hold true in all cases.

The fourth major hypothesis, often referred to as the cerebellum hypothesis, has been developed by Angela Fawcett and Rod Nicolson (2004). In essence, they believe that the cerebellum – which plays a crucial role in integrating different streams of information as well as in relaying this information to the rest of the brain – may be underperforming in dyslexics. Because of this, learning takes longer. They also believe it accounts for the poor balance experienced by dyslexics.

Once again, this theory is not without its critics (see Ramus *et al.* 2003). There is evidence that some dyslexics have an underperforming cerebellum, but not all do. I am far from convinced that the cerebellum hypothesis applies universally to all dyslexics, since the proportion of dyslexics who excel at sports is relatively high (see Chapter 6). Having met dyslexics who are national champions at ice-skating, cycling and gymnastics – all sports that require excellent balance – a difficulty with balance is not a universal dyslexic trait. I believe, however, that it is possible to reconcile these very different approaches. Fundamental to all of them is some form of weakness in information processing. It is possible that this occurs at a very basic level.

For information processing to take place, incoming streams of information have to be broken down into small bits of information, which are then reassembled to give them meaning. For example, when listening to someone talking, it is as if the brain breaks the continuous stream of information down into small chunks of information every 130 milliseconds. However, there is some evidence that in cases of dyslexia the chunks are larger – perhaps about 210 milliseconds in length (Helenius *et al.* 1999). There may also be a similar type of difference in visual processing. It has been shown that, at the first memory stage of visual information processing, the time it takes for an image to decay and disappear, which is usually just milliseconds, is shorter for dyslexics (Ben-Yehudah *et al.* 2001). As the very brief visual images decay faster than expected, this results in the brain experiencing some difficulties with comparing the last image with the current one. It's as if the picture is slightly cloudy.

Although these four major theories about dyslexia appear at first sight to be quite different from each other, there is one theory which can unite all of them – the asynchrony hypothesis of Michel Habib (2000). A significant feature of Habib's way of thinking about dyslexia is that it encompasses dyspraxia as well. His ideas about the underlying basis of dyslexia are important, for he has proposed that the tempo of information processing may be different in dyslexics.

If we assume that the brain works best when all neuronal systems are in synchrony with each other, difficulties will arise if one system is running very fast or very slow compared with the others. There are many different systems in the brain, including the major ones of vision, language and movement. If the time-coding of information processing is impaired between these three systems, then both dyslexia and dyspraxia are likely.

If just one system is affected it might give rise to a visual or verbal form of dyslexia. In principle, it is possible to see how slow timing in one system gives rise to difficulties when integration between systems is required. If the auditory timing is slow, then the matching of sounds with images will be problematic and will result in slowness with some forms of learning.

This concept of processing systems needing to run at 'the right pace', as it were, also applies to the creation of memories. For memories to become permanent it is necessary for the nerve cells of the brain to fire at the right tempo and in the right sequence (Fields 2005). If visual or auditory processing systems are not operating at the same rate – that is, they are asynchronous – this is likely to have a knock-on effect in that long-term memory is also affected.

It appears to me that Michel Habib's approach not only encompasses all four of the current major theories of dyslexia, but also goes beyond them, since it embraces dyspraxia as well as dyslexia. What most theorists overlook is that dyslexia and dyspraxia are not separate conditions. I have found that about 30% of the students I see are dyslexic and dyspraxic – to differing degrees. Many experts on dyspraxia claim that the overlap is even higher. Because there is such an overlap, I suggest that we can only claim to understand what dyslexia is when that explanation encompasses dyspraxia as well.

Chapter 3

What is Dyspraxia?

When carrying out a diagnostic assessment I always ask the question, 'Were you well-co-ordinated or clumsy as a child?' In a surprisingly high number of cases the reply is, 'I was clumsy – still am.' Clumsiness and difficulties with motor co-ordination are classic soft signs of the presence of dyspraxia. When these difficulties are severe enough to result in a clumsy child being diagnosed as being dyspraxic, a physiotherapist or occupational therapist will then work with that child to bring about improvements in motor co-ordination. In some cases speech therapy is required as well. However, it is a mistake to assume that improvements in motor control and speech result in a 'cure' for dyspraxia. The underlying cognitive characteristics, a big part of being dyspraxic, are still very much the same and are often ignored. In addition, many people are never diagnosed as being dyspraxic in the first place. For example, Laura has lived with being clumsy throughout her life but has just accepted this as being part of her: 'I have learnt to live with who I am.'

Dyspraxia is similar to an iceberg in two ways. Firstly, there is a small visible part with a very considerable hidden portion. The visible part in the case of dyspraxia is the element of clumsiness and associated difficulties with motor co-ordination. The hidden aspect is the underlying difficulties with attention, memory and some tasks requiring perceptual skills. The second similarity is that, over time, the visible part becomes smaller and less noticeable. This gradual melting away analogy refers to the observation that co-ordination skills improve over time and people also learn to become 'more careful'. Consequently, as a child grows into a teenager and then an adult, the visible aspects of being dyspraxic often become quite muted. However, in spite of it appearing as if clumsiness has gradually 'melted away', other key aspects of dyspraxia do not change with time.

The most obvious aspect of being dyspraxic is clumsiness and this is summed up in the phrase 'clumsy child syndrome'. Clumsiness can take different forms, such as bumping into things, knocking things over, spilling things and tripping over your own feet. As it is demeaning, as well as age-inappropriate, to refer to a teenager or adult who is clumsy as having 'clumsy child syndrome', the term 'dyspraxic' is much more frequently used.

However, some writers and clinicians draw a distinction between being dyspraxic and having developmental co-ordination disorder. The key difference between these two diagnostic labels is that dyspraxia is said to be present when an individual experiences difficulties with the cognitive planning for carrying out a skilled motor act, whereas someone with developmental co-ordination disorder is able to carry out the cognitive planning but cannot execute that plan due to lack of motor control. That is, a person with developmental co-ordination difficulties will 'know what to do but does not do it very well' (Kirby and Drew 2003: 6).

While it is theoretically possible to distinguish between dyspraxia and developmental co-ordination disorder, in practice it is often hard to distinguish between these two diagnostic labels and most people in the UK use the term 'dyspraxia' to cover both. As with dyslexia, I believe it is more helpful to talk about the dyspraxias than dyspraxia, as it can take different forms. I strongly suspect that there are more than two forms. However, rather than worry about how many labels there should be, I believe it is much more important to focus on the profile of an individual's strengths and weaknesses. In my view, the use of the Wechsler Intelligence Scales is essential to drawing up that profile. This battery of tests can bring into full view many of the hidden aspects of dyspraxia.

This point can be illustrated by describing two students I have seen. John was first diagnosed as being dyspraxic when he was seven. Amanda was not diagnosed as being dyspraxic until she was in her early twenties. John's birth was a very difficult one and he was a floppy baby (rather like a rag doll – his legs and arms flopped about). As he had not stood up by the time he was 18 months old, he was provided with physiotherapy to help him learn to walk. He was also a very messy eater. Although he was walking by the time he started school he could not climb steps and was consequently provided with further physiotherapy. It was not until he was seven that a consultant finally diagnosed him as being dyspraxic.

What is striking about John's case is how long it took for his parents to be given a diagnosis. As this can take so long, even when motor co-ordination difficulties are evident from so early on, it is easy to understand why children with more subtle forms of co-ordination difficulties are not identified at all.

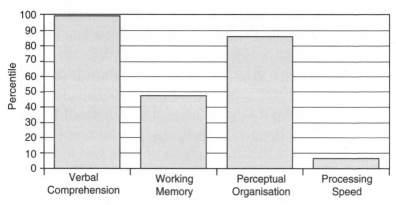

Figure 3.1 John's four WAIS Index scores expressed as percentile scores

When I met John he was studying English Literature at a highly respected university. His assessment (see Figure 3.1) revealed a very high level of verbal reasoning ability – the top 0.1% of the population. His visual reasoning abilities, although 'high average', are well below his exceptionally high verbal reasoning performance. Of the three visual reasoning subtests he took, his lowest score was on the Block Design subtest, a test of being able to think three-dimensionally. A dip in performance on this subtest is a typical dyspraxic feature. There is a working memory weakness and John's speed of visual processing is exceptionally low – the bottom 5% of the population.

Although John's visual reasoning performance is comfortably above average, his sense of place and space is nevertheless very poor. It takes him very much longer than most people to learn how to find his way around a building or area, and he still gets lost in places he has known for some time. John is prone to lapses in concentration and his writing style is typically dyslexic, in that he finds it hard to structure essays and writes sentences that are very long and complex, with poor punctuation. This is in spite of his having excellent skills of spelling and word reading accuracy. His reading speed is a little below average.

As a child John experienced some difficulties with learning to read and he disliked having to read aloud in secondary school as he had some problems with pronunciation. He has always found it hard to get to sleep.

Many of John's experiences are common to dyslexia and constitute part of the hidden side of dyspraxia. Until his assessment John had not been aware that these experiences are dyspraxia-related. The Dyspraxia Foundation defines dyspraxia as 'an impairment or immaturity of the organisation of movement. In addition, there may be problems of language, perception and thought.' These are all reflected in John's description of himself. (These thought characteristics are due to a weak working memory and refer to such behaviours as daydreaming and going off at tangents.)

John's difficulties with motor co-ordination were clearly evident from his earliest months. Amanda's difficulties were more muted. There are many similarities between John and Amanda. Their WAIS profiles are very similar, except that Amanda scored lower on Working Memory (see Figure 3.2). Like John, her word reading accuracy and spelling skills are excellent, whereas her speed of reading is below average.

Amanda was a 'blue' baby and began walking a little late. She was always 'bumping into lampposts' as a child and still bumps into people. She disliked sports at school as she could not catch or throw. She tried to learn a number of musical instruments but eventually settled on the flute, as it required less co-ordination than the guitar or piano.

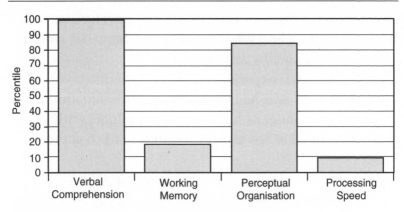

Figure 3.2 Amanda's four WAIS Index scores expressed as percentile scores

Amanda took a degree in Life Sciences but struggled with some of the practical activities such as drawing while using a microscope, and with titration. (This activity requires a flask to be swirled with one hand and a tap turned on and off, quite gently but swiftly, with the other.)

Amanda has always learnt slowly, especially when rote learning was required and she chose options on her degree that were assignment-based, even though it took her longer than other students to write essays and reports. In order to be organised she has to write herself lists of things to do. She is easily distracted when engaged in activities such as reading or writing.

Although Amanda initially sought an assessment because of the study difficulties she was experiencing, the more subtle problems she had with motor co-ordination only came to light when she was asked a series of questions about her personal history. Amanda's case is important, since it raises the serious question of whether dyspraxia is the appropriate diagnosis for her. If the American standard is followed, then such a diagnosis can only be applied when there is a marked impairment in motor co-ordination and this has a significant adverse effect on academic achievement or the activities of daily life. The American approach avoids saying anything about other associated aspects, such as weaknesses in memory, attention and perception.

Although Amanda's difficulties with motor co-ordination are not marked, they have had an impact on a range of activities, such as avoiding having to take part in sports, influencing which instrument she could learn and asking her university laboratory partner to carry out titrations on her behalf. She has genuine continuing difficulties with co-ordination but, compared with John's, they are muted. They are also much less obvious as she has learnt to be more careful. On the other hand, her cognitive profile is a very spiky one and this has impacted negatively on her experiences at school and university and colours her everyday life. Because the definition of the Dyspraxia Foundation is more holistic than the American approach in that it captures the cognitive as well as the motor co-ordination aspects of being dyspraxic, the most appropriate diagnosis for Amanda is dyspraxia. Amanda is typical of many who have been affected by dyslexic-type experiences without being dyslexic, and not known why school, university and work have posed so many challenges.

Whereas John's and Amanda's profiles are very similar in many ways, there are other types of profiles. The profile for Cathy (see Figure 3.3) is one also typically encountered in instances of dyspraxia. The most obvious difference from the profiles of John and Amanda is that Cathy's performance on visual reasoning is below average and is on a par with her score for speed of visual processing. (In my experience, a low score on Perceptual Organisation is often associated with difficulties with maths, and Cathy required three attempts before she passed a national maths exam.)

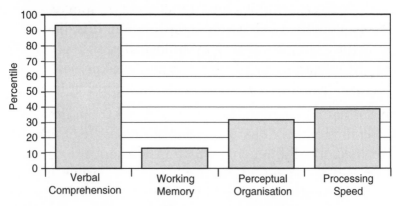

Figure 3.3   Cathy's four WAIS Index scores expressed as
percentile scores

Cathy's birth was free of complications. She recalled
always dropping things as a child and, as an adult, she
has a tendency to bump into things. She struggled with
learning handwriting skills and tying her shoelaces and
she still has trouble with zips. Cathy is accident-prone
and broke her arm and her leg in separate accidents in
her teens.

When Cathy was at secondary school she was placed
in the top groups for all subjects except needlework.
Cathy said she was unable to thread a needle. Her school
would not let her enter a national art exam. Cathy
recalled often forgetting to take items she needed to
school and her teachers often mentioned that her written
work was poor in terms of planning and punctuation.
Her difficulty with organising ideas when writing essays
became so debilitating that, although Cathy completed
first a degree and then a Master's course, she felt that her
'academic self-confidence' had been destroyed. It was
not until she had a diagnostic assessment that, for the
first time, she was able to understand why she had
consistently underperformed throughout her education
and was able to make sense of her everyday experiences.

All three case-studies reveal that being dyspraxic affects more than just motor co-ordination. It is, like dyslexia, a complex neuropsychological profile of significant variations in strengths and weaknesses. Because there are so many shared similarities, it is not surprising that, in my experience at least, I see more people who are both dyslexic and dyspraxic than are purely dyspraxic.

As with cases of undiagnosed dyslexia, the constant struggle to achieve at school and university often erodes self-confidence. Even skills that dyspraxics become good at, such as reading and spelling, often take them longer than others to learn. In many cases, being poor at sports further erodes self-confidence, particularly if this is accompanied by bullying.

The case histories of Amanda and Cathy are typical of many dyspraxics I see, in that their difficulties with motor co-ordination are not sufficiently severe for a clinical opinion to be sought. There are times when you wonder just how severe this has to be. For example, I have spoken to one student who was only referred for a clinical opinion when his infant school teacher recognised that his constant falling off his chair at school was due to lack of motor control.

Nevertheless, the signs of problems with motor co-ordination were plainly evident from childhood and have shaped their lives. Being dyspraxic, even when the motor elements are relatively muted, does affect lives and influence career choices. For example, only about 5% of students I see are Art and Design students. However, of the students I see from what are regarded as the UK's top universities, one-third are dyspraxic. Intuitively you would expect that dyspraxic students would experience some difficulties with art- and design-type subjects. As they often have very considerable verbal skills, and in many cases good or excellent mathematical skills, it would be anticipated that dyspraxics are more likely to choose to study such subjects as the humanities and sciences at university.

In comparison with dyslexia, dyspraxia is grossly under-researched. It is my opinion that the underlying causal mechanisms are the same or similar to those encountered in dyslexia. However, the trigger in some cases appears to be a difficult birth. It is possible that the neurological processes serving working memory and processing speed are particularly vulnerable to factors that stress the brain, such as a difficult labour. It is known that close brain injuries, such as occur following a motor car crash, affect both working memory and processing speed. This points towards the relative fragility of these neurological systems. There is also evidence that, when the brain is subjected to stress, right-hemisphere functions are affected more greatly than left-hemisphere ones. The higher score for verbal than visual reasoning often observed in many cases of dyspraxia is indicative of a stronger left hemisphere.

In conclusion, there are probably even more unanswered questions about the dyspraxias than there are about the dyslexias. What we can be sure of is that the defining feature of dyspraxia – difficulty with motor co-ordination – is the tip of the iceberg. Psychologists need to work in conjunction with physiotherapists and occupational therapists to ensure that dyspraxics are given access to the full, complex picture.

Chapter 4

Colours and Reading

'It's just like a bra – it lifts and separates each word.'
Surprising as it may seem, Sonia's comment reveals how
an overlay of just the right colour can change the visual
appearance of a page of text in unexpected ways. When
Sonia placed the coloured overlay that was the right
colour for her over a page of text she immediately
noticed that she could see the individual words much
more clearly. Without the overlay the words looked as if
they were clumped together, and she had to tease out
each word from the others around it when reading.
Consequently she read aloud in a hesitant manner.
However, as soon as she placed the overlay that best
suited her over the text, the words appeared to be
separate from each other – 'the words look like words'.
Her reading speed improved and she felt more relaxed
and confident.

Sonia's experience is not unusual. Roughly 40% to
50% of the dyslexics and dyspraxics I see report a very
noticeable and positive improvement in the visual
perception of text when using the coloured overlay they
find is best suited to them. For most, this comes as a
major surprise. Most people find it difficult to describe
what a page of words in a textbook or novel looks like to

them before they try out a range of different coloured overlays. However, when they compare the appearance of a page of words with and without using the overlay that is the best colour for them, they are surprised by the difference. That is the point when they suddenly realise that words don't have to 'dance around on the page', 'clump together' or 'pop up out of the page', and they don't have to be 'swamped by the glare of the white of the page'.

Many dyslexics and dyspraxics, without knowing it, experience visual stress when reading words printed in black on white paper. (This is why this book has been printed on a tinted paper.) This stress increases with decrease in the size of print. This may be one key reason why some people, who enjoyed reading when young, gradually stop reading for pleasure as they enter their teens. Children's books are generally printed in a large typesize. However, as stories increase in complexity, print size decreases and an underlying visual stress factor then becomes more of an obstacle to the enjoyment of reading.

Visual stress also affects the reading of music. When this visual stress factor is present, people often tire very quickly, whether reading words or music, and lose their place easily. Reading is not a pleasure – it has to be worked at – because the eyes are darting about. Eye movements are not smooth and controlled: 'It is as if the corner of my eye picks up a letter from somewhere on the page and flicks it into the word I'm reading.'

When this visual stress is present it can be overcome with the right coloured overlay, or the right coloured background when working at a computer monitor. (The software ReadAble enables an individual to set the background colour to the colour that suits them best. See Appendix.) There is no one colour that works for everyone. Usually the colour that is best for an individual is a very specific one. For some lime-green is the most effective colour, for others mint-green. For others aqua works, while blue doesn't.

It is only relatively recently that this positive impact of coloured overlays has been discovered (and some say rediscovered). Two people, working independently of each other, are credited with this discovery – Helen Irlen in California and Colin Meares in New Zealand. That is why this visual stress syndrome is often referred to as the Meares-Irlen Syndrome. There are also alternative names; for example, Helen Irlen (1991) named it Scotopic Sensitivity Syndrome. However, most people nowadays prefer the name Meares-Irlen Syndrome.

Although their research was highly controversial in the years immediately following the publication of their findings, many people – but not all – have since accepted that Meares-Irlen Syndrome does exist and that coloured overlays help to offset it. (The most effective overlays have a slightly frosted appearance on one surface.)

There is a major difference between demonstrating that coloured overlays offset visual stress and understanding the reason why they are effective. What is certain is that when visual stress is present it occurs because of poor co-ordination of eye movements. Secondly, we know that eye movements are controlled by the cerebellum (this is an area at the back of the brain that functions rather like an air traffic control centre). When reading, the eyes need to make very fast and very precise movements. They have to feed back information about the words to be read next as well as the word that is currently being read, so they have to scan forwards and backwards quite smoothly.

When Meares-Irlen Syndrome is present, this smoothness is absent. Why this is so, and why colours help, is not fully understood. My interpretation is a simplistic one but captures the essence of what is probably happening. The cerebellum is linked to the retina (the light-sensitive cells at the back of the eye) by two major pathways: the magnocellular pathway and the parvocellular pathway. The magnocellular pathway carries mainly back and white information and works very fast. The parvocellular pathway mainly carries colour information from the retinal cells to the cerebellum and is slightly slower.

We know that, in some dyslexics, but not all, the magnocellular pathway is short of magno cells. This will then break up the smooth flow of information to the cerebellum. When this happens, it is as if the cerebellum is trying to control the eyes in a fog. This results in an increase in mental energy being required, while eye movements become unfocused and dart about. However, when the right coloured overlay is found, information is redirected to the parvocellular pathway. Although this pathway is slower, the flow of information becomes smoother and more complete. It is as if the cerebellum now has a better picture because the fog has lifted and many more words can be seen. There is greater separation between the words and the lines of text – the 'bra' effect. Stress levels go down and speed of reading goes up.

If it was just a question of switching to the parvo pathway, then any colour should help. As this is not the case, another factor – colour pigment – has to be considered. The back of our eyes contain a mixture of very specialised cells, some of which play a crucial role in helping with colour recognition. Some cells have a blue pigment, some a red one, and yet others have a green pigment.

Crucially, the proportion of the red and green pigments varies from person to person. We know that four different genes control the production of the red pigment, and another four genes control the production of the green pigment. Consequently, there are subtle differences in how individuals respond physiologically to the same colours. Hollingham (2004) summed it up very nicely: 'We all live in our own sensory world.'

This aspect of individuality is very important. While the available evidence suggests that everyone benefits to some extent from using a coloured overlay, for most people the improvement is very minor. However, for some people – mainly dyslexics and dyspraxics – the benefit is greater; for some, it's much greater. It is important to stress that Meares-Irlen Syndrome is sometimes observed in people who have no specific learning difficulties at all. I have also observed it in people who are colour-blind. It is also independent of a sensitivity to light, a factor that affects some people.

Very occasionally, the impact of Meares-Irlen Syndrome is so strong that an individual will feel nauseous and lose balance just by looking at a page of words. This was the case for Judith. Meares-Irlen Syndrome was present to such an extent that doctors wrongly diagnosed her as being epileptic and she had to give up work. Once she had been identified as being dyslexic with extreme Meares-Irlen Syndrome and been provided with the coloured overlays that best suited her, she enrolled on a journalism course and began, in her mid-fifties, to successfully fulfil her lifelong ambition. When Meares-Irlen Syndrome is present in a moderate or severe form, the solution can quite literally be life-transforming. Coloured overlays do not resolve most dyslexic or dyspraxic issues, but they can and do remove a significant barrier for a number of people.

Chapter 5

Becoming Creative

When asked whether being dyslexic had influenced his photography, the world famous photographer, David Bailey replied: 'I feel dyslexia gave me a privilege. It pushed me into being totally visual.'

www.Showstudio.com 12 February 2003

There is a powerful public perception that being dyslexic means you are likely to be creative. If you look at the website of the British Dyslexia Association there is a long list of famous dyslexic people. Most of those named are well-known for being creative, including Lord Richard Rogers (architect), Eddie Izzard (comedian), Lynda La Plante (scriptwriter) and Benjamin Zephaniah (poet). Over 85% of the famous names listed on the British Dyslexia Association website have made their mark in professions that we associate with being creative, such as the arts, design, music, writing and the media. There are virtually no scientists, engineers or business people in the list.

It has been known for a long time that the proportion of students who are dyslexic and are studying art or design is much higher than for other subjects such as business studies or the sciences. As success in art and design is related to being creative, does this imply that dyslexics are more creative than non-dyslexics? A number of people believe so.

Lord Laird, speaking in the House of Lords on 8 May 2000, made the claim that 'Lateral thinking, problem solving, the ability to make creative leaps and see things from every angle are all skills associated with dyslexia.' The dyslexia.com website explains that dyslexia is a gift because 'Dyslexic people are visual, multi-dimensional thinkers. We are intuitive and highly creative.'

I'm not so sure that dyslexics are born to be creative, visual thinkers. I suspect that it is the experience of *being* dyslexic that leads to many dyslexics becoming creative, and *being* dyslexic that influences their choice of which profession to enter.

Surprising as it may seem, remarkably little research has examined the assumed link between being dyslexic and being creative. There is very extensive research on creativity. There is very extensive research on dyslexia (but much less on dyspraxia). However, very little research has been carried out that looks at both dyslexia and creativity together. I suspect it is this lack of research that has allowed the myth to develop that being dyslexic means you must be a creative visual thinker as well.

It is worth reading David Bailey's comment again. 'I feel dyslexia gave me a privilege. It pushed me into being totally visual.' Note his use of the word 'pushed'.

It is intuitively easy to understand how an association between dyslexia, art and creativity has arisen. If you experience problems with reading, spelling and maths, and with expressing your ideas in writing, success in many subjects becomes difficult to achieve, no matter how hard you try. Subjects such as art, design and technology, which are more practical and require less reading and writing than most other subjects, therefore become attractive. Consequently, when dyslexic school pupils get a chance to choose which subjects they want to study, they tend to opt for these subjects. Art and design are also perceived as being the more creative subjects. The choice made at school then tends to restrict the subjects that can be studied at undergraduate level, which in turn influences career options.

This is what I call the 'least barriers' route. The same thing happens in the sciences and engineering as well. Many dyslexic and dyspraxic science and engineering students tell me they particularly enjoy the practical aspects of these subjects and that they find writing reports much easier than writing essays because reports have a clear structure. Many dyslexic and dyspraxic students therefore decide to specialise in science or engineering because there are fewer barriers to success than if they were to choose humanities or social science subjects.

However, it is important to note that, as science and engineering require good mathematical skills, this excludes a number of dyslexic and dyspraxic students. Whereas some find maths easy, others find maths very difficult. As the arts and most design areas do not require mathematical skills, the least barriers principle will again apply, and some students will find themselves being pushed towards these subjects.

Although I have met a number of students who would automatically have chosen art, design or the sciences irrespective of whether they were dyslexic or not, I have also met students who have felt pushed towards these subjects because they presented fewer barriers to success. This push towards art and design is much more powerful for someone who is dyslexic than for someone who is dyspraxic.

In the case of a person with classic dyspraxia, reading and spelling levels are in harmony with the level of verbal reasoning, so subjects such as English and History don't appear intimidating. In addition, the typical dyspraxic features of a poor sense of three-dimensional visualisation and weak fine hand–eye co-ordination will affect skills of drawing and painting. These two factors are likely to discourage someone who is dyspraxic from specialising in art or design.

When I first began carrying out dyslexia diagnoses for students studying art or design, I expected to find these students would have a level of visual reasoning that was at least as good as their verbal reasoning, if not better. In practice, the opposite is often the case. I have been surprised by how many art and design students have scored higher on Verbal Comprehension than on Perceptual Organisation. I had not expected this at the time, but it may be surprisingly easy to explain.

I suspect there are two key factors at play here. First, there is the least barriers factor. That is, as described above, some students go on to study art and design, not because there are naturally inclined to these subjects, but because they sense they will do better in them than subjects that require good reading and writing skills. Second, the study of art and design has changed considerably over the past decade and now embraces a range of new skills as well as the more traditional ones.

For example, installation art has become a medium that a number of students now choose to specialise in. Installation art draws on non-traditional art skills such as sound design and video production. Consequently, a dyslexic art student who thinks verbally rather than visually can be successful on a Fine Art degree by electing to work with installations. The same applies to students of broadcasting. Just like art and design, broadcasting encompasses a wide range of specialisms. Some aspects of broadcasting, such as camera operation, lighting and set design, are very visual. Other aspects, such as scriptwriting and presenting, are strongly verbal. Being stronger at verbal than visual reasoning is not the obstacle to success in art it would have been some years ago.

So far we have discussed the push factor as one reason why there are likely to be more dyslexic students taking art and design than other subjects. To succeed as an artist or designer you also need to be creative. It is said by a number of people that being creative is a dyslexic strength. I feel this might be the case for some dyslexics – but not all – although not for the reason usually given.

Before explaining this further, it is useful to look at what makes for successful creativity. Most researchers agree on two key aspects. First, creativity is about finding original solutions that are effective. The key point about this definition is that there is equal emphasis on both originality and effectiveness. Novelty or newness for its own sake doesn't count. The solution must also work.

Second, being creative is a basic human trait. Without an ability to be creative we would be robotic and unable to undertake such basic activities as speaking and thinking. Being creative is not reserved for those we call geniuses. Being creative is what we all do every day. That does not mean, however, that we all have the same level of creativity. Some people are more creative than others.

There are several reasons for this. Although it would be wrong to discount natural differences in creative ability between people, it is possible to learn techniques to become more creative. We can also work harder at achieving creative solutions. This aspect of working harder may seem a little unusual, but in fact research has shown that it is often the critical factor as to why some people succeed to a greater extent than others.

Arriving at an effective creative solution is not just a matter of waking up one day and knowing the answer to a question. This stage in the problem-solving process is known as illumination. To reach this point requires two previous stages: preparation and incubation. Preparation is about identifying what the question should be as well as researching possible avenues to explore and gathering relevant information. Incubation describes the process of leaving a question ticking over in the back of your mind, and it follows on from the preparation stage.

The stage of preparation is influenced enormously by the amount of hard work that is put into this stage. When the life history of creative achievers is examined, this factor stands out. For example, when the painter Turner was asked for advice about painting, he replied: 'The only secret I have is damned hard work.'

The researcher Ochse captures this aspect of hard work perfectly in her quote, 'before the Gates of Excellence the High Gods have placed sweat – the sweat of labour – often mingled with the sweat of pain' (1990: 132). If there is one unifying factor running through the accounts of people who are creatively successful, it is this capacity for hard work.

Most dyslexic and dyspraxic students I have seen mention how much more effort they have to put into their assignments and university work to just get the same grade as their fellow non-dyslexic and non-dyspraxic students. Because they know it takes them longer than others to research and write essays, they start work much earlier than others and all aspects of the process take longer, perhaps three or four times as long. It is therefore highly likely that this sets up a persistent work habit that is particularly beneficial in creative endeavours.

We can see this commitment to hard work in the comment by Peter, a dyslexic ceramics student, who told me, 'my attitude is, because of who I am, I got into a habit of working much harder and thought, if I was going to compete, my efforts would have to be higher and that doesn't stop – whatever I do, whether it's written, physical or creative'.

There are other key factors that might be at work as well. Studies of the life histories of creative achievers (Ochse 1990) reveal that many saw themselves as being different from other children, and they often received considerable encouragement from their parents. I have been struck by the number of dyslexic and dyspraxic students who have voiced their feelings of being different from other children. Emma's statement captures the childhood experiences of a number of dyslexic and dyspraxic students I have met: 'I was certainly different, certainly – I remember feeling different . . . I used to spend a lot of time on my own and I did things on my own. . .I used to go home and cry.'

Very often these students have enjoyed the support of at least one parent who has realised that they are struggling and has tried to be as supportive as possible. When Emma talked about her parents, she said, 'He always encouraged me, my mum always encouraged me, she always read to me . . .'

If we put these three factors together – the need to work harder than others, feelings of being different and supportive parents – we can see that the formative years for a dyslexic or dyspraxic child help to shape a way of thinking and behaving that fosters being creative. In other words, it is the experience of being dyslexic or dyspraxic that is important for becoming creative, not the dyslexia or dyspraxia itself.

Having said that it is the experience of being dyslexic or dyspraxic that is important, other possible contributory factors to being a creative thinker should not be totally discounted. For example, brainstorming is a technique that many students are taught to help them generate ideas. This technique is often used as a starting point when a brief is given out. It has previously been suggested that a limited working memory capacity results in ideas slipping in and out of conscious thought in an almost random manner. This results in a transient and chaotic experience – almost like an ongoing brainstorming session.

As a weak working memory often results in people going off at tangents, more unusual associations of ideas tend to be formed. Emma, a Fashion student, was well aware of just how quickly her mind jumps around: 'Everything around you is inspiring, music from passing cars, faces at bus stops . . .' This type of 'brainstorming' experience, which results from the limited capacity of conscious auditory memory, is therefore more likely to throw up more unusual combinations of ideas, with the consequence that unplanned solutions have more chance of occurring.

This may be a significant factor in helping someone to arrive at a new way of thinking about a question. Although this may help at the initial stage of problem-solving, it can sometimes be a distraction. Some students find it very difficult to stay focused on their main idea as they work towards the end product, because they keep going off at tangents. Peter, a ceramics student, was familiar with this experience: 'There are so many ideas you have to be selective. Once I cast a vessel, I have a thousand ideas from it.' Peter knew that one of his strengths, the ability to generate lots of ideas, could also become a liability unless he kept it under control.

Because some dyslexic students find they can be side-tracked so easily, they prefer to select subjects with an in-built structure. Sarah, a composer and drummer, spent a year on a Photography degree course before changing to a degree in Popular Performance Music. Because composing has a clear structure to it (you lay down the drums and bass parts before adding the parts for guitar, keyboards and lyrics), she felt much more at ease. She told me that 'structure has always been quite important – I find structure helped me quite a bit and I find without it I'm sometimes a bit lost – I need to do a lot more work without it'.

The limited capacity of auditory working memory may also force a reliance on other sensory memories, such as visual, tactile and kinaesthetic ones. We can see this factor at work in Sarah's comment: 'I can hear the sounds and maybe hear it in the vocals as well, but also when I'm hearing rhythm in songs I'm always imagining it physically and visually as well – that can help me remember.'

Sarah's use of imagining rhythm physically and visually is partly driven by the ease with which she forgets things. 'I had a really great idea, it's gone – it's the best idea I've had and it's gone . . . it's like grrrr . . . when I don't write things down and it's a good idea and it's gone, it's frustrating.'

For many students, a better technique than just writing ideas down when trying to organise them is to map ideas visually. For example, I remember showing a student how the mind-mapping software Inspiration can be used to capture ideas in a visual form. After using it for a couple of minutes he said, 'That's the way I think.' Because of his very limited working memory, he found he needed to capture and organise his ideas visually. That way, he could see all his ideas together.

For some dyslexics and dyspraxics who have become proficient at visual thinking, this becomes their preferred way of thinking. I emphasise the word 'some', for not all dyslexics and dyspraxics are visual thinkers, but are much more comfortable thinking verbally, even with its limitations.

A weak working memory may also contribute in quite an unusual way to creative thinking. The chapter on sleep (Chapter 8) reports that many dyslexic and dyspraxic students have difficulty getting to sleep. During this time many find themselves going over and over things that happened during the day and things they need to do. Consequently, this often involves thinking about a brief they have been given. For some students this can be their most creative thinking time.

Being creative frequently involves bringing together very different sets of information. Whereas this can be difficult in the daytime because of other competing demands for attention, the stillness of night ensures there is a greater chance of the necessary elements coming together. Because getting to sleep, for some, can take so long, there is an even greater chance of an appropriate solution being arrived at. This can be viewed as an enforced opportunity to work harder than the non-dyslexic or non-dyspraxic person. However, there is little point in arriving at the perfect solution only to forget it by morning. This is the reason why some students have a 'night book'. If they have a good idea while trying to get to sleep, they immediately write it down. They can then relax knowing they have 'captured' their idea.

This additional time for creative thinking at night may be important in that, for some dyslexics and most dyspraxics, speed of visual processing is often a weak point. This factor affects speed of learning. Creative thinking is a stage process. The beginning stage, preparation, requires research which usually involves the acquisition of new facts, ideas, techniques, even questions to ask. This takes time.

A slow speed of visual processing, allied with a weak working memory, slows down the rate at which someone who is dyslexic or dyspraxic can learn. So reaching the point at which a creative solution can occur may be a slower process than for a non-dyslexic or non-dyspraxic student.

It is important to note that, even if all the preparatory work has been undertaken, not everyone will arrive at an effective creative solution at the same time. This slowness often results in many dyslexics and dyspraxics knowing that they are capable of high-quality work, but needing to proceed at their own pace. This is reflected in their dislike of having to work under pressure.

This factor of slowness of processing speed is an important one for some art and design students, as in some instances it will be reflected in drawing style. Many art and design courses still require drawing skills. Some people can draw rapidly and fluidly, putting down confident lines, but not everyone can do this. In the case of someone who has a high level of visual thinking, but a slow speed of visual processing, it's as if their brain is thinking faster than their hand can execute an idea. This can then be reflected in a style of drawing that consists of smaller strokes, lines that overlap, and fainter marks. This style of drawing may look scratchy, or hairy. For example, Hannah described her drawing style as being scratchy.

Some courses, such as Fashion, place an emphasis on fast sketching (for example, when making sketches of models on catwalks and creating roughs). Tanya is a very gifted Fashion student. However, when given a

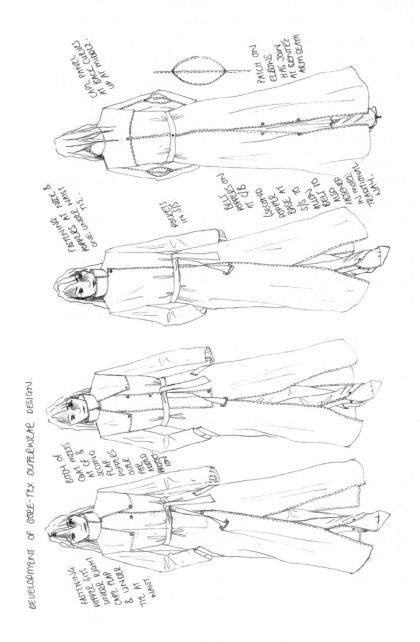

DEVELOPMENT OF GORE-TEX OUTERWEAR DESIGN.

CAPE PANEL CURVES UP AT MIDDLE.

PATCH ON ELBONS HAS JOIN AT CENTRE ARM SEAM

FASTENING AT NECK & POPPERS AT WAIST ONE UNDER TIE.

POCKETS IN S/S

BELT POPPERS ON AT C/B (SECOND POPPER BASE AT S/S TO ALLON TO BELT ALSO FASTENED IN MORE TRADITIONAL WAY.

BODY OF COAT RISES AT CF & SECOND FLAP POPPERS OVER FOR ADDED PROTECTION

FASTENING POPPER SITS UNDER RIGHT CAPE FLAP & UNDER TIE AT WAIST.

67

brief and asked to produce a number of roughs, she was unable to work at the same speed as other students. Whereas her fellow students could produce about 12 rough sketches of their initial ideas in an hour, Tanya was only able to produce about four. In addition to sketching slowly, she described her sketches as having a wooden feel to them, as she lacked fluency. Yet by the time she had completed a design brief, her finished garments were first class.

Tanya, Hannah, Emma, Peter and Sarah are typical of many dyslexic students. They are talented, hard-working and quite individual. As the quotes above illustrate, they think and work in different ways. This individuality is important for it reveals that the process of being creative takes different forms. This makes generalisation difficult. Just as there are various types of dyslexia, there are different creative processes. Arguably the common feature is the relationship between being successful and hard work.

It is also important to note that the arts and design are not the sole provinces of creativity. All aspects of employment require people who are creative. Although relatively few people will have heard of Guy Hands, he is a dyslexic City of London financier who has a world-wide reputation for developing innovative funding methods.

Rather more people will have heard of Richard Branson. He is dyslexic and is renowned world-wide for spotting new opportunities and developing new services. The Virgin group of companies differ radically from most others. It is interesting to speculate whether the eclectic Virgin group of companies might be a reflection of a dyslexic mode of thought. Anita Roddick, founder of The Body Shop, is another famous dyslexic who has been very successful in business. Her dyslexic daughter, Sam

Roddick, has more recently also made her mark by creating the Coco de Mer chain of shops.

Being dyslexic means experiencing childhood and the teenage years in a different way from non-dyslexics. It would be surprising if this was not then reflected in what a person becomes and elects to do.

Chapter 6

Sports, Genes and Evolution

Dyslexia is at least as old as mankind. This may appear to be an amazing claim to make but this chapter goes from known facts to thinking 'outside the box'. This chapter explores some questions that are overlooked or ignored in almost every book on dyslexia. The first of these questions is: Why should dyslexia be so widespread?

I live and work in London, where the mixture of cultures and races is extremely diverse. Consequently, I see students from many different countries. To give you some idea of this diversity, I have carried out diagnostic assessments for students from China, Iceland, India, Iran, Israel, Kuwait, Malaysia, Nigeria, Russia and Uganda. In spite of very different languages and writing scripts, there are very striking and uniting factors. Each student experienced significant difficulties with learning to read and spell at school. Every student has always had problems with memory in spite of good verbal reasoning skills, and they are all slow at processing visual information. This universality of typical dyslexic characteristics did not come as a surprise to me, for I was quite familiar with pioneering cross-cultural research into reading difficulties carried out by Stevenson *et al.* (1982).

This research was carried out in three countries – America, Japan and Taiwan. In each country the researchers assessed the performance of a representative, general sample of ten-year-old schoolchildren by measuring reading ability as well as verbal and visual reasoning skills. In each country they identified children who had reasoning skills below expectation. The percentage of children with unexpected reading difficulties in all three countries was approximately the same – around 6%.

This research was very important, as it demolished the myth that dyslexia is not found in children taught to read and write in Japanese or Chinese. That is, in spite of very different writing scripts, approximately the same number of American, Japanese and Chinese children still experience unexpected difficulties with learning to read. This research also demonstrated that in cultures where there is no word for dyslexia, dyslexic children are considered to be responsible for the difficulties they experience because they are not working hard enough. For these students it is very hard for them to explain to their parents what being dyslexic means.

What are the implications of dyslexia being found in all national groups? Imagine walking into a room that contains six dyslexic students, each from a different country. There is a Chinese student and the others are from Kuwait, Kenya, the West Indies, Sweden and Pakistan. The obvious racial differences would be immediately striking but there would be no way of knowing any of them were dyslexic unless they mentioned it or you had been informed beforehand. However, in spite of such obvious physical differences, their neuropsychological profile would be the same.

To observe such a similarity in spite of very different physical racial characteristics can only mean one thing in evolutionary terms – being dyslexic predates the point at which racial differences began to evolve. In evolutionary terms dyslexia appears to have been present since the beginning of mankind.

The only other interpretation is to argue that there is some environmental factor common to all cultures that triggers the development of dyslexia. For example, could diet be such a factor? I'm not convinced that this line of argument stands up to close scrutiny as a good general explanation of why dyslexia occurs. For example, the diet of a student born in the UK, but whose parents are from Afghanistan or Iceland, might be different from the diet of his or her grandparents. However, if you then discover that one of their grandfathers or grandmothers is suspected of being dyslexic, it is highly likely that the grandparent's diet was very traditional. In other words, in spite of changes in diet across generations, dyslexia is a constant.

When considering the proposal that diet is an important factor in helping to explain why dyslexia occurs, it is important to stress that there is a big difference between rejecting diet as a *good general explanation* and allowing for some exceptions.

The question of diet is currently important in that some researchers have argued that our current intake of an important fatty acid, Omega-3, which is vital to brain function, is much lower than it was several centuries ago. However, this line of argument overlooks the fact that dyslexia is present in both Japan and Iceland, two countries with a high consumption of fish, which is a very important source of Omega-3. The inescapable facts are that dyslexia is widespread and the incidence appears to be roughly the same across countries. What is more, it is known to be hereditary.

As a generalisation, if you are dyslexic there is a 1 in 2 chance that each child you have will also be dyslexic.

As you will know by now, dyslexia is quite a complex condition. Because of this complexity, and because the inheritance factor is not a straightforward one, most geneticists (for example, Fisher and DeFries 2002) are in agreement that dyslexia is an expression of a combination of genes rather than there being a single dyslexic gene. (It is, in fact, very unusual to find a one-gene, one-condition association. What strikes most geneticists is how complex things are, not how simple. For example, eye colour is determined by at least nine genes.)

Recently, geneticists have discovered a new level of complexity. Genes can be switched on and off by what are known as histones. Histones are a special kind of chemical messenger that influence how hard genes have to work at creating proteins – from not working at all to going into overdrive. What this new level of complexity means is that three people can have the same gene, but for one person that gene may be switched on and working at just the right level; for another the gene might be working but only slowly; while in the third person the gene may be switched off.

In theory, this means that what you eat, drink or take in from your environment could in some way potentially influence histone production. So it is just possible that diet may be a factor. If it is, it is likely to influence the action of a couple of genes at the most, not the complicated combination of genes that underlie being dyslexic.

To date the most compelling evidence that fatty acids are important for some people comes from the research of Richardson and Montgomery (2005). They have reported improvements in reading skills and spelling performance – but not motor co-ordination – in dyspraxic school children given fatty acid supplements over a three-month period. In about one-third of cases, ability to pay attention also noticeably improved.

Because of this genetic and histone complexity, making predictions about whether a child with a dyslexic parent might be dyslexic is fraught with difficulties (and dyslexic gene screening is a long way off). Current prediction is based on probabilities, which means that, while it is highly likely that some children with a dyslexic parent will be dyslexic, not all children will be. Because of the complex nature of dyslexia, the severity and type of dyslexia will also vary within a family.

As dyslexia is known to run in families this enables an intriguing question to be addressed – would it be possible to be dyslexic in a preliterate society? Education for all children within a given society is a very recent development. Only about 150 years ago education was for the privileged few, even within almost any of today's developed nations. So, could one of your ancestors have been dyslexic 150 years ago if they had not been taught to read and write? For example, if you are dyslexic, and your mother or father is dyslexic, could you then discover that your great-, great-, great-grandfather or -mother was also dyslexic even though they never went to school? 150 years is only about six generations.

The answer depends entirely on how dyslexia is defined. If the only criterion is that verbal reasoning abilities are significantly higher than reading and spelling skills in spite of adequate education, then dyslexia cannot exist in someone who has not formally been exposed to the teaching of reading and writing. This definition does, however, then give rise to a developmental problem – dyslexia cannot exist in preschool children either. How, then, can someone be diagnosed as being severely dyslexic at the age of eight or nine, but be said not to be dyslexic when they are about three or four?

If a broader definition of dyslexia is used, then a child can be dyslexic at the age of six months as well as the age of three years, or eight or 15. Broader definitions include unexpected difficulties with reading and spelling as being just one facet of being dyslexic. Other aspects typically affect memory and concentration, and a slow speed of visual processing, and these would be expected to be present from birth. In principle, it should therefore be possible to diagnose someone as being dyslexic or dyspraxic soon after they are born.

Because some of the key neuropsychological features of dyslexia are shared with dyspraxia and Attention Deficit Disorder or Attention Deficit Hyperactivity Disorder (ADD/ADHD) as well, care would have to be taken when carrying out a diagnosis on a young child to distinguish dyslexia from dyspraxia and ADD/ADHD. Just as an infant can therefore be said to be dyslexic before starting school, so also can it be stated that dyslexia existed in preliterate societies.

This is not such a radical proposal as it may seem. Andrew Ellis (1985) voiced the opinion that, whatever dyslexia might eventually turn out to be, it would almost certainly be found to have little to do with reading or spelling.

The ability to remember and to forget is fundamental to human survival. Without being able to remember, everything would be a new sensation. Without an ability to forget, we would be swamped with information. The ability to remember and forget is a basic survival process for animals as well. In evolutionary terms, the ability to remember and forget must have evolved at a very early stage in the development of animal life. In spite of this, these processes are still little understood, other than being known to be very complex. This complexity is a strong indication that they must be genetically complex as well.

As with the inheritance of any process that is known to be complex, significant variation is to be anticipated. This is in fact the case. I have encountered students with photographic memories; I have met a student who has difficulty recognising the face of her own child; I have come across students whose working memory is so weak that remembering three consecutive numbers is almost impossible; while others can recall virtually nothing of their childhood. Significant variation between all types of memory, whether that be visual memory, working memory or long-term memory, is a feature of human life.

Because a very poor memory can be so disruptive to everyday life, it would be anticipated that evolutionary pressures would favour the survival of those with the best memories. This pressure would have been exerted over many millennia, for a tendency to forget what you have just set out to do, to daydream more than others, or to have a difficulty with organisation or learning quickly, would arguably be a disadvantage in almost any society, whether nowadays or 100,000 years ago.

If evolutionary pressures favour the survival of those with an effective memory, then why is a weak working memory such a prominent feature of many dyslexics? To answer this question requires speculation and, in order to address it, I will explore the evolutionary line of thought a little further. I will then take what may appear to be, at first sight, a very unusual approach by talking about the relationship between sports and dyslexia and dyspraxia.

There is no doubt that a weak working memory is a source of frustration for many dyslexics and dyspraxics. It is, however, just possible that long ago in our evolutionary past a weak working memory might actually have been an advantage rather than a disadvantage. This advantage might have come about because there is a strong tendency for people with a weak working memory to be easily distracted.

Many dyslexics and dyspraxics often describe themselves as easily losing concentration. In general, the greater the working memory deficit, the more easily distracted someone will be. This is a major disadvantage if you are working in a library, an office or studio, or at home, if every time you hear a noise or sense a movement you look up from what you are doing. This ease of distractibility, would, however, have been a major advantage half a million years or more ago, for our brains have evolved to enable us to survive in an uncertain and dangerous world.

A constant fear of our ancestors living half a million years ago would have been as ending up as lunch for a hungry animal. Under such circumstances, being extremely alert and very sensitive to sudden movement or unexpected noises would have been an important survival mechanism. This kind of behaviour is evident when you watch a bird or squirrel feeding. It may well have been the case that those individuals who were the most easily distracted were those who had the greatest chance of escaping being eaten.

However, as our ancestors evolved, social rules and language would also have emerged and become more complicated. These changes could only have come about if they had also been accompanied by increases in working memory, for it is working memory that is the hub of our sense of consciousness and deliberation. Evolutionary pressures would therefore have favoured the development of memory processes, including working memory. But this pressure would have been pulling against the much older pressure of distractibility being an advantage.

Although the association between ease of distractibility and survival would have been a very powerful survival mechanism some millennia ago, I don't think it has entirely disappeared. Those individuals who are best suited to an environment are those most likely to survive and pass on their genes. Sensitivity to the unexpected would be an important characteristic. So would physical prowess. This takes me to the next stage of my thinking 'outside of the box'.

Over the past four years I have assessed many students who have achieved a very high level of sporting achievement. These students include a world sailing champion, a European champion in Taekwondo, a UK cycling time trial national champion, a UK national cross-country runner, a Malaysian national swimming champion, a Chilean bronze medallist in gymnastics and a Swedish bronze medallist in free-style skating. These students – four men and three women – are all dyslexic.

For some years now I have asked all the people I see questions about their attitude to sport and sporting ability when building up a personal history profile. I do this because it helps to distinguish dyspraxics from dyslexics. As a rough generalisation you would anticipate that dyslexics would enjoy sport at school because it provides an escape from subjects involving reading and writing. On the other hand, it would be expected that dyspraxics would dislike sports because of the need for good co-ordination skills.

As ever with the understanding of dyslexia and dyspraxia, the reality is more complicated. Some dyslexics hate sports. Some dyspraxics are enthusiastic about sports and reach a high level. For example, Ryan, a

12-year-old school child, is dyspraxic and the Sussex judo champion for his age group.

It is very important to keep in mind that enthusiasm for sports is not the same as being good at sport. Enthusiasm is, however, very important because of its motivational aspect. Being dyslexic or being dyspraxic brings with it certain challenges. For example, a weak working memory results in difficulties with those sports that require multitasking.

As an example, consider all the different elements that have to be thought about when learning to play netball. These include remembering which area of the court to stay within – move outside this and you give away a penalty. You also have to think about ball control, which way you are playing and where your team-mates are. You also have to try and take note of what they are saying or indicating. Because you have to take account of so many things simultaneously, you need to be able to multitask to be a good player, especially when learning the game. It is not surprising that dyslexics and dyspraxics find they tend to give away more penalties than others.

In general, team sports such as netball require more in the way of multitasking than individual sports such as running or swimming. The rules are often complex and there is a need to pay close attention to what your team members, as well as the opposition, are doing. For example, I have met rugby players who have reached a high level but have always frustrated their coach and team members because they cannot remember the line-out calls. (These are usually in code so that the opposition cannot work out who the ball will be thrown to.) One rugby player described how the team captain would stand behind him in the line-out and tell him when to jump, as he could never remember these codes.

An analysis of the data I have collected from the dyslexic and dyspraxic students I have seen reveals that they are more likely to choose, and then succeed at a high level, in individual sports such as swimming and track athletics than in team sports such as football, netball and basketball. It is therefore not surprising that the students I have seen who have reached a national or higher level of success all participate in individual sports. It is also not unexpected that Hannah's illustration reveals her sport to be judo – another individual sport.

Hannah's illustration also reveals that, like many dyslexic and dyspraxic students who enjoy sport, she

has to work harder at succeeding. Even when a dyslexic or dyspraxic prefers to play in a team sport, I have noticed a tendency for them to play in defence. If you think back to a typical neuropsychological profile for dyslexics and dyspraxics, visual reasoning skills are generally better than speed of visual processing. That is, there is a good ability to read the game but a lack of the swiftness of response that is the hallmark of a striker. However, once again it is wise to avoid applying a generalisation to all dyslexics or dyspraxics. Sir Jackie Stewart is dyslexic. He is also a world Grand Prix Formula One champion.

Not all dyslexics and dyspraxics enjoy sport. For some, particularly dyspraxics rather than dyslexics, early attempts at taking part in sport and PE at school are so humiliating that they eventually give up and often seek to avoid having to take part in PE or games at school. The humiliation of being the last to be picked for a team, especially when you are desperate to play; the bullying that is often experienced by those who are poor at sports – serve to erode self-confidence and self-esteem.

Of those dyslexic students who enjoy taking part in a sport, a surprisingly high proportion go on to be really good at it. Of the dyslexic students I have assessed, 13% have excelled at some aspect of sport. I have used as a measure of excellence whether a student has been chosen to represent their county at one or more sports, and used equivalent measures for overseas students (such as representing a province in France, Land in Germany or state in the USA). To be selected to represent a county or equivalent in a chosen sport, it is necessary to have reached a high level of sporting performance. Of the dyslexic students I have seen over the past three years, 13% have represented their county at one or more sports. This figure of 1 in 8 is much higher than would be expected in a typical UK university population. How, then, can this finding be explained?

There is an obvious answer and an alternative, more complicated explanation. The obvious reason is that sport represents an escape from the classroom for a number of dyslexic students. Therefore, these students will be highly motivated and devote more time to their chosen sports. This line of argument assumes that enthusiasm plus practice leads to excellence. However, I have seen too many people fail to be selected to represent their county even though they have the motivation, and practise year after year. Another factor that is required for success is natural ability.

The next stage of the argument represents a speculative leap in thinking, for I'm now going to put forward the complex explanation. If 1 in 8 dyslexic university students have excelled at a sport, this implies that there is a link, even if only a tenuous one, between being dyslexic and being good at sports. It is far from being a one-to-one association, but it occurs at above chance level.

If this link exists, then excellent physical skills are precisely the kind of attributes that would have been advantageous in just about all societies and throughout the ages. In other words, such individuals would have had a head start in most societies. In evolutionary terms, such individuals would have been favoured and this would cancel out the downside of being dyslexic. It is highly likely that individuals with excellent physical skills would have gained power and prestige in most societies, particularly if they were male.

We know from anthropology and history that men with power and prestige are likely to have more than one wife or female partner. Because of the inheritance factor this would result in the dyslexic gene clusters being widely distributed – among the most powerful and influential families of the time. Perhaps it is more than an interesting fact that I know of three royal families with dyslexic members.

There is one further twist to this line of speculation. Approximately one-third of dyslexic students report a complication with their birth, such as a long and difficult labour, prematurity, or delivery by Caesarean section. However, whereas 1 in 3 dyslexic students report some form of birthing complication, only 1 in 15 male county-level dyslexic students report such a complication. Somehow a complication-free birth seems to be linked with sporting ability.

This link can be considered in historical terms. Giving birth in the past was a very dangerous activity, partly because of poor diet, and partly because of lack of midwifery expertise. However, the wives of the powerful would have enjoyed a better diet than most – thus having a bigger gap in the pelvic bone for a baby's head to pass through, and would have had access to the best available midwifery assistance. Thus the incidence of birthing complications is likely to have been lower than for the wives of the general male population. This factor would therefore have played a part in ensuring the continuation of physical prowess – and the dyslexic gene pool.

I started off this chapter by stating that I would move from known factors to thinking 'outside the box' and I have advanced the proposition that dyslexia has a very long evolutionary history. Given that being dyslexic is associated with some negative factors, such as a weak working memory, there has to be a powerful reason why it has survived over millennia and across nations. The answer may be because it is, unexpectedly, associated in a tangential way with high levels of physical prowess and our evolutionary past. This is a speculative line of reasoning – some would say, 'way outside the box'. However, there is still much we don't know about dyslexia, and many questions remain to be answered.

Chapter 7

'Invisible' Girls and Women

There is a long-standing myth that many more males than females are dyslexic. It may also be a myth that many more males than females are dyspraxic. For a number of years I believed these to be true but, about five years ago, I changed my mind about there being about three to four times more dyslexic males than females. There were two simple but powerful reasons for this change of opinion: I began meeting many more dyslexic women than men who had not previously been diagnosed, and I came across recent research which challenged this myth about dyslexia. I am not the only one to have changed my mind. For example, the website of the UK government's Department for Education and Skills draws attention to the idea that dyslexia may affect both sexes equally (www.dfes.gov.uk, 7 May 2005).

Over the past five years I have carried out diagnostic assessments for more than 1,000 students. Very early on I was struck by two things. First, more women than men were referred to me for a diagnosis. Second, for every two men I saw and diagnosed as being dyslexic for the first time, I was seeing three women for whom this was their first diagnosis. More recently, when I looked at my data for dyspraxic students, this type of discrepancy was even higher. To date I have seen more than twice as many women than men who had not previously been diagnosed as being dyspraxic. Because my figures run so contrary to expectation – I anticipated seeing about three or four times as many dyspraxic men as women – it could only mean one thing. My figures suggested that girls who are dyslexic or dyspraxic are much more likely than boys to escape being diagnosed at school.

In order to discover why so many girls missed out on being diagnosed while at school, I listened to what students told me about their school experiences. Whereas some themes were common to both sexes, such as difficulties with concentration and being told, 'You need to try harder', some comments occurred with much greater frequency for girls than boys. Many females described themselves as working much harder than other girls and taking care not to draw attention to themselves. Sharon spoke for many when she described how she tried to make herself invisible in class: 'I sat at the back of the class and hid behind the biggest girl in front of me.' She also tried to avoid catching the eye of the

teacher. Farrah was typical of many who tried to avoid being asked questions in class: 'I tried to hide behind my books, I tried to sink into my desk'. Like many undiagnosed dyslexic and dyspraxic students, Sharon and Farrah cut back on activities such as sports, music and social life in their mid-teen years to enable them to concentrate much more on their school work.

It has been my impression that a girl's sense of self-esteem is much more damaged than a boy's by having unexplained difficulties at school. This damage often begins in primary school when everyone else appears to understand what they have to do.

This feeling of being both different and inferior can then be compounded by being told off by the teacher for asking too many questions and being teased by other pupils for not being very bright. At secondary school this trend to a lowering of self-esteem is fed by being placed in low sets and increasing difficulties with homework. At this point avoidance strategies are adopted, such as asking to go to the toilet to avoid being asked to read aloud in class, or feigning illness to avoid going into school altogether. It is not surprising that some of the mature students I see found themselves pregnant when they were in their late teens. For some it is a new start towards rebuilding self-esteem.

Once again, as a rough generalisation, boys appear to adopt a different set of strategies in response to difficulties with academic work. When John described how he became 'the joker' in his year, he spoke for a number of boys. It was his way of distracting the other boys' attention from his real academic difficulties. In a number of cases male students have described how they became disruptive in class. Probably the extreme case was Tony. He described how he became so frustrated at being told off by his maths teacher for not doing his homework that he hit the teacher. Following his suspension from school he was assessed and found to be severely dyslexic. His local education authority then arranged for him to go to a boarding school that specialised in teaching dyslexic pupils. Tony said this was 'the best thing that happened to me'. Other boys find that sporting activities provide them with an outlet that gives them status at school, an outlet that is less attractive to many girls.

I am not the first to suggest that the different ways in which boys and girls respond to difficulties result in boys being noticed while girls fade into the background. In 1999, Wagner and Garon described the outcome of a longitudinal survey that followed a group of American schoolchildren from kindergarten to graduation. Over this period of time children with reading difficulties were identified in two different ways. When teacher reports were used as the basis, about three times as many boys were identified as having reading difficulties as girls. However, when a research approach was applied and all children were assessed, the numbers of boys and girls with reading problems were almost equal. The study concluded that 'the difference in the prevalence of reading disability between boys and girls appears to be an artefact of referral bias. Boys tend to be more disruptive than girls and consequently are more likely to be referred. . .' (1999: 89).

This observation, that a research approach to the identification of reading difficulties results in finding almost as many girls as boys as having reading problems, is matched by an almost identical finding from a major survey that used a research approach across three countries – the USA, Korea and Japan. (This work of Stevenson *et al.* is also referred to in Chapter 6.) Explanation of gender differences based on the impact of male hormones on the developing brain, or the influence of the male X chromosome (see Jones 2002) would appear to be – at the least – open to serious questioning.

Trying to determine gender differences on the basis of counting how many males and how many females have been referred for assessment has always been known to be a potential source of error. That is why I have been very cautious about my own data. However, because UK colleges and universities have become much more proactive and positive about providing support for students with a range of specific learning difficulties, undiagnosed students have – often for the first time – had an opportunity to disclose their genuine difficulties, difficulties that they have often hidden from many people. The invisible are slowly becoming visible.

There is still a long way to go and, if dyslexia is a hidden learning difficulty, dyspraxia is even more hidden. It is also my experience that dyslexia is even more invisible in children with English as an additional language. While it is easy to attribute a child's difficulties with learning to read and spell in English as being due to his or her family using Polish, or Chinese, or Urdu at home, close questioning often reveals, in the case of dyslexia or dyspraxia, a cluster of typical behaviours and experiences, such as a tendency to be forgetful, or slow at writing. Dyslexia and dyspraxia do not respect gender or nationality. Cultural expectations, whether of gender or ethnicity, can hinder rather than facilitate the search for the true situation.

While it is very important to be aware of the power of gender-based beliefs, it would be misleading to leave the impression that this is the sole reason why more girls than boys are not diagnosed as being dyslexic. There is another factor at work. Even at birth girls are biologically advanced compared with boys, and this difference widens over the years. By the time of puberty – a word that literally means 'to become hairy' – this biological difference is one of more than 12 months. However, the publishers of tests do not take account of this difference. Instead of calculating an average score for girls, and another average score for boys, they calculate an average without taking sex into account. Consequently, the average girl will perform better on a test than an average boy. This in turn means that more boys will score below average, and there will be more boys in the lowest scoring groups. Consequently, if a teacher relies just on class tests, more boys will appear to be at risk than girls.

Biology, combined with gender-related cultural expectations, masks the genuine difficulties that dyslexic girls experience at school. I suspect that the same factors are at work for dyspraxic girls as well.

Chapter 8

Sleep

Which statement best describes you?

- When I go to bed and close my eyes, I usually fall asleep quickly.
- When I go to bed and close my eyes, I have difficulty getting to sleep because my mind buzzes with thoughts.

In general, only about 1 in 4 university students report frequent difficulties with getting to sleep. However, when dyslexic students are asked whether they fall asleep quickly, about 60% to 65% report having problems. That is, about two to three times as many dyslexic students report frequent difficulties with getting to sleep as non-dyslexic students.

When I asked Hannah to draw an illustration that captured this feature of dyslexic life, she immediately knew what I was talking about. She is dyslexic herself and also has trouble getting to sleep. As you can see in her illustration, she also keeps a notebook by her bedside – something that at least 1 in 6 dyslexic students do. They do this because they know that if they don't jot down an important idea as soon as it occurs to them, they are likely to forget it by the following morning.

Difficulty with getting to sleep has previously been reported as being a characteristic of dyspraxics but not, as far as I know, of dyslexics. Why, then, has this been overlooked? It probably stems from the very definition of dyslexia. Most definitions of dyslexia are very narrow as they concentrate on either reading and writing or phonological processing. They do not concern themselves with the everyday experiences of being dyslexic. The consequence of this narrow definition is a narrow approach to research. Virtually all research on dyslexia focuses on language and literacy, while the more general aspects of being dyslexic are ignored.

However, the definition of dyspraxia is much broader. Consequently most books about dyspraxia take a much more holistic approach and it is easier to form a more rounded picture of the individual.

In order to gain an understanding of what it is really like to be dyslexic, it is necessary to spend time exploring wider aspects of everyday life. Ever since listening to a dyslexic student talk about her difficulties with getting to sleep about three years ago, I have made a point of asking all the dyslexic students I see about their experience of getting to sleep. The common history of a difficulty with falling asleep emerged almost immediately. When asked what thoughts and ideas occurred during the period of time before drifting off to sleep, a majority described how they use the time to sort through the day's events and plan for the following day.

They often point out that ideas, sometimes good or important ones, just 'pop' into their minds. They also frequently say that, because they know they have difficulties with remembering, they take steps to write these ideas down, even though they are in bed, because they know that otherwise they would have forgotten the idea by the time they wake up the following morning.

Very often they mention they feel more relaxed having noted an idea down. Not everyone keeps a notepad by the side of their bed. Some students use their mobile phones as organisers, and one student described how helpful she found it to have a whiteboard at her bedside. As she had previously written ideas down on scraps of paper, which she then lost, she knew she could not lose the whiteboard.

The second most common theme that students report is creative thinking. However, in comparison with the numbers who mention 'sorting through the day's events and planning for tomorrow', thinking creatively is much less prevalent. Creative thinking is also, for some students, interlinked with thinking through the events of the day if they have spent the day working hard on an assignment.

For some students, getting to sleep can take so long and is so disruptive that they have experimented with different strategies to help them fall asleep. A common technique is to play a favourite CD 'I've heard a thousand times before' to help blot out ideas. Other strategies include watching a film on television, using meditation, drinking camomile tea and having a warm bath. Surprising as it may seem – to a non-dyslexic – reading rapidly induces sleepiness in some dyslexics. Therefore, some students deliberately start reading to help them fall asleep. There does not appear to be a magic technique that will work for everyone. What works for some people, such as playing a CD, keeps others awake.

Why is it that so many dyslexics and dyspraxics find it difficult to get to sleep? The fact that it occurs for both groups provides a clue, for common to both is a weak working memory. This night-time thinking period for dyslexics and dyspraxics is frequently taken up with sorting through the day's events and planning for the following day: 'What did he/she mean when they said that?', 'Have I got time to do that tomorrow?', 'I must not forget to do that'. Ideas and thoughts 'pop' into consciousness at random, sometimes only for a fleeting moment. A short poem by Sue captures this experience perfectly.

> As I lie awake in bed
> Poems come floating through my head.
> I try to grasp them, grab them, catch them,
> But somehow I just can't nab them.

If you listen to a dyslexic or dyspraxic describing their thought patterns when they are trying to get to sleep, at times it sounds very much as if their mind is trying to restore order to chaos. To help understand what is going on, it is helpful to consider the role of working memory.

Working memory is a mental survival process. It enables us to bring into consciousness memories of past events as well as thoughts about the future. It enables us to be aware of what we have done as well as what we could do. It is vital to survival. When someone has an active life but a working memory deficit, working memory will be overworked throughout the daytime. As a consequence, it is as if many thoughts don't get processed and there is a backlog of unfinished work by the end of the day.

At bedtime there is a sudden drop in external stimulation. It's much quieter and it's dark. Because of this drop in external stimulation, working memory can begin to function more effectively and this enables unfinished business from the day to be resolved. It is a form of mental clearing up.

Although this analogy has a simplicity to it that appears to capture what is going on, it is unlikely to be the whole story. Another factor to consider is stress. A weak working memory and a slow speed of visual processing will impede the rate of learning. This immediately places dyslexic and dyspraxic students at a disadvantage when they are required to work and learn at the same pace as other students. Stress will give rise to anxiety, which, in turn, will affect the ease with which someone can fall asleep. Although stress should not be discounted as an important factor, dyslexics' and dyspraxics' descriptions of what they think about suggest that thoughts about sorting through the day's events and planning for the following day are much more frequent than the type of thoughts that would be typical of someone under a high degree of stress.

It is important to remember that not all dyslexics and dyspraxics have difficulties with getting to sleep, and about 25% of the general undergraduate population has trouble getting to sleep. Also, a small minority of dyslexics and dyspraxics do not consider that taking an hour or more to fall asleep is a 'difficulty'. Typically, they have always spent considerable time thinking before falling asleep, and believe this must be the case for everyone else as well. Nevertheless, the frequency with which dyslexics and dyspraxics report difficulties with getting to sleep reveals that this is an important but overlooked feature of being dyslexic or dyspraxic. A number of dyslexic and dyspraxic students experience this difficulty throughout their life and a few find it quite disruptive. A surprising number of dyslexic students report staying up late – and often say they are the last one in their student flat or house to go to bed because they know that getting to sleep will be such a long process. Consequently, getting up then becomes a problem.

When I first presented my survey revealing dyslexics' difficulties with getting to sleep, a tutor, who was herself dyslexic, carried out a brief survey of her dyslexic colleagues. She was amazed to discover that, like herself, they all said they had problems getting to sleep, and they all kept a notebook by their bedside. Not one of them had appreciated that this was a typical dyslexic characteristic.

At the end of telling me about her mini-survey, the tutor asked a very pertinent question: 'How much more is there to discover about the experience of being dyslexic?'

Chapter 9

Concluding Remarks

'I have learnt to live with who I am.' When Laura described herself in these words she spoke for many undiagnosed dyslexics and dyspraxics. Throughout her life she had known she did some things differently from many other people, and found some things difficult that others found easy, but she had never known why. At the end of her assessment, and following a discussion of how her profile of strengths and weaknesses was reflected in her personal history, it was as if an enormous burden had been lifted from her. She was still the same person, but now, at long last, she had an explanation.

My motivation to write this book came from meeting many people like Laura. Because being dyslexic or dyspraxic shapes, colours and influences so many aspects of everyday life, it is appropriate to describe being dyslexic or dyspraxic as really being a lifestyle. Consequently this book covers a number of different aspects of everyday life and provides explanations for them.

For example, difficulties with memory are frequently observed in both dyslexics and dyspraxics and affect a wide range of experiences, such as remembering where you have just placed an item, taking in information in a briefing and remembering the names of people you have just met. A weak working memory also creates difficulties with determining the order of ideas in an essay or report and with sentence structure. More surprisingly, problems with remembering may also help explain why so many dyslexics and dyspraxics have trouble getting to sleep. From the time of waking up to the time of falling asleep, dyslexia and dyspraxia influence how many aspects of daily life are experienced.

It is not, therefore, unexpected that this shapes the kind of careers dyslexics and dyspraxics select. The chapter on being creative develops a new way of thinking about why dyslexia and creativity are often linked together. Being creative requires long spells of hard work. Dyslexics – and dyspraxics – are so used to having to work harder than others that it is not surprising that this degree of commitment successfully spills over into the workplace.

In providing explanations it has, at times, been necessary to dispel myths about dyslexia and dyspraxia. For example, if we believe that dyslexia and dyspraxia are predominantly associated with being male, then dyslexic and dyspraxic girls and women are likely to be overlooked. I have presented evidence that reveals that dyslexia and dyspraxia are more common in females than many have believed, and have sought to explain why this gender bias has occurred.

More controversially, ideas concerning the universal nature of dyslexia and its evolutionary history have been explored. It is proposed that being dyslexic is an experience that, many millennia ago, was a survival advantage, and this factor may account for why dyslexia and sporting prowess are linked.

Of all the ideas explored in this book, perhaps the two most important are that it is much more helpful to recognise the different forms that dyslexia and dyspraxia take, and to realise that dyslexia and dyspraxia are more similar than dissimilar. This then enables us to recognise people's individuality and arrive at explanations that make sense. Through understanding comes liberation. Laura spoke for so many when, at the conclusion of her diagnostic assessment, she said, 'I can now put my demons behind me and plan for a new future.'

Appendix: Suppliers of Assistive Software

There is a wide range of assistive software now available. There are frequent updates of current software. New products are introduced on a fairly regular basis. Most assistive software is not available from high-street shops. There are two major web-based suppliers in the UK:

- www.dyslexic.com (Be very careful when typing out this web address, as it is 'dyslexic', not 'dyslexia'.)
- www.Microlinkpc.co.uk

References

Ben-Yehudah, G., Sackett, E., Malchi-Ginzberg, L. and Ahissar, M. (2001) 'Impaired temporal contrast sensitivity in dyslexics is specific to retain-and-compare paradigms.' *Brain*, **124**, 1381–95.

Boder, E. (1973) 'Developmental dyslexia: a diagnostic approach based on three atypical reading-spelling patterns.' *Developmental Medicine and Child Neurology*, **15**, 663–87.

Ellis, A.W. (1984) *Reading, Writing and Dyslexia: A Cognitive Analysis.* London and Hillsdale, NJ: Lawrence Erlbaum Associates.

Ellis, A.W. (1985) cited in Wolf, M. and O'Brien, B. (2001) 'On issues of time, fluency, and intervention', in Fawcett, A. (ed.) *Dyslexia: Theory and Good Practice.* London: Whurr Publishing, p. 124.

Fawcett, A.J. and Nicolson, R. (2004). 'Dyslexia: the role of the cerebellum', in Reid, G. and Fawcett, A. (eds) *Dyslexia in Context: Research, Policy and Practice.* London: Whurr Publishers, pp. 25–47.

Fields, R.D. (2005) 'Making memories stick'. *Scientific American*, **292**(2), 59–65.

Fisher, S.E. and DeFries, J.C. (2002) 'Developmental dyslexia: genetic dissection of a complex cognitive trait.' *Nature Reviews: Neuroscience*, **3**, 767–80.

Grant, D. (2002) *The Dyslexias and Diagnostic Issues in Higher Education*. Northampton: National Association of Disability Officers (NADO).

Habib, M. (2000) 'The neurological basis of developmental dyslexia: an overview and working hypothesis.' *Brain*, **123**, 2373–99.

Helenius, P., Uutela, K. and Hari, R. (1999) 'Auditory stream segregation in dyslexic adults.' *Brain*, **122**, 907–13.

Hollingham, R. (2004) 'In the realm of your senses.' *New Scientist*, 31 January, **181**, 40–2.

Irlen, H. (1991) *Reading by the Colors*. New York: Avery Publishing Group.

Jones, S. (2002) '*Y: The Descent of Men*'. London: Little, Brown & Company.

Kirby, A. and Drew, S. (2003) *Guide to Dyspraxia and Developmental Coordination Disorders*. London: David Fulton Publishers.

Ochse, R. (1990) *Before the Gates of Excellence: The Determinants of Creative Genius*. Cambridge: Cambridge University Press.

Ramus, F., Rosen, S., Dakin, S.C., Day, B.L., Castellote, J.M., White, S. and Frith, U. (2003) 'Theories of developmental dyslexia: insights from a multiple case study of dyslexic adults'. *Brain*, **126**, 841–65.

Richardson, A.J. and Montgomery, P. (2005) 'The Oxford-Durham Study: A randomised, controlled trial of dietary supplementation with fatty acids in children with Developmental Coordination Disorder.' *Pediatrics*, **115**, 1360–6.

Schonell, F.J. (1945) *Backwardness in the Basic Subjects*, 2nd edition. Edinburgh and London: Oliver & Boyd Ltd.

Smythe, I. (2005) On being dyslexic in one language but not another. www.barringtonstoke.co.uk/teachers/ newsletter05b, 13 February.

Snowling, M.J. (2000) *Dyslexia,* 2nd edition. Oxford: Blackwell Publishers.

Stein, J., Talcott, J. and Witton, C. (2001) 'The sensorimotor basis of developmental dyslexia', in Fawcett, A. (ed.) *Dyslexia: Theory and Good Practice.* London: Whurr Publishing, pp. 65–88.

Stevenson, H.W., Stigler, J.W., Lucker, G.W. and Lee, S. (1982) 'Reading disabilities: the case of Chinese, Japanese and English.' *Child Development,* **53,** 1164–81.

Wagner, R.K. and Garon, T. (1999) 'Learning disabilities in perspective', in Sternberg, R.J. and Spear-Swerling, L. (eds) *Perspectives on Learning Disabilities: Biological, Cognitive, Contextual.* Oxford: Westview Press, pp. 83–105.

Wolf, M. and O'Brien, B. (2001) 'On issues of time, fluency and intervention', in Fawcett, A. (ed.) *Dyslexia: Theory and Good Practice.* London: Whurr Publishing, pp. 124–40.